IMAGES
of America

A Journey through
BOSTON
Irish History

Heavyweight champion John L. Sullivan was interred at Old Calvary Cemetery in 1918, and this grand obelisk marks the final resting place of the great fighter. (Photograph by Greg Cecconi.)

IMAGES
of America

A JOURNEY THROUGH
BOSTON
IRISH HISTORY

Dennis P. Ryan

ARCADIA

Published by Arcadia Publishing,
an imprint of Tempus Publishing, Inc.
2 Cumberland Street
Charleston, SC 29401

Printed in Great Britain.

Library of Congress Catalog Card Number: 99-62237

For all general information contact Arcadia Publishing at:
Telephone 843-853-2070
Fax 843-853-0044
E-Mail edit@arcadiaimages.com

For customer service and orders:
Toll-Free 1-888-313-BOOK

Visit us on the internet at http://www.arcadiaimages.com

The cadets of the Catholic Boston School for the Deaf muster for a group photograph, 1908.
(Courtesy of the Boston School for the Deaf.)

CONTENTS

This map shows the 32 counties of Ireland. The Irish on arriving in Boston often clustered in neighborhoods with people from their own local village and county.

INTRODUCTION

A thriving seaport community of some 114,000 inhabitants, Boston was inundated in the 1840s by thousands of starving, destitute Irish immigrants fleeing the Great Famine. A watershed event in modern Irish history, the potato blight was caused, as scientists would discover some years later, by a fungus known as *phytophthora infestans*, which began in the autumn of 1845 and ravaged Ireland for the next five years, sweeping away more than 1 million men, women, and children and forcing 2 million others to seek refuge in British Canada and the United States. In Boston the Irish huddled in tenements and damp cellars in the North End and in shanties on Fort Hill near the waterfront, their wretched poverty overwhelming city public health officials and appalling the native Yankee population. In 1847, a year in which 35,000 emigrants alone arrived in the Hub, "groups of poor wretches were to be seen in every part of the city," noted the *Boston Transcript*, "resting their weary and emaciated limbs at the corner of the streets and doorways of both private and public houses."

"The Irish have always been very unpopular in this city," observed Thomas C. Grattan, the British consul to Boston in the 1840s. In 1834, when Boston's pre-famine Irish Catholic colony numbered a mere 5,000, a mob descended on the Catholic Ursuline Convent in Charlestown, ransacking the interior, making a pyre of holy books and crucifixes, and desecrating the Holy Eucharist before finally torching it to the ground. In the 1850s the infamous anti-immigrant Know-Nothing party, campaigning under the banner "Put None but Americans on Guard," disbanded Irish militia companies, pestered Catholic schools throughout Massachusetts, and tried to thwart naturalized citizens from voting. In Boston newspapers it was not uncommon to find advertisements for employment stipulating, "Irish Need Not Apply."

The Irish started at the bottom of Boston's economic ladder, working as teamsters, stable hands, coachmen, gardeners, and as laborers on railroads springing up across Massachusetts. Self-reliant, adaptive, and mostly single, thousands of young Irish women toiled as domestics and cooks in the handsome mansions of wealthy Beacon Hill and Back Bay Brahmins, selflessly sending part of their earnings back home to pay the passage of their brothers and sisters.

While materially poor, the Irish were abundantly rich in religious faith. In Boston, a bastion of Protestantism, the first Catholic church, the Cathedral of the Holy Cross, located at the eastern end of Franklin Place, was dedicated in 1803. In the wake of the Great Hunger, the Catholic church expanded rapidly in Boston, as Bishop John Bernard Fitzpatrick noted to an intimate in 1864, because of "the faith, piety and zeal of our good Irish Catholics." The parish church was the social and cultural as well as spiritual center for generations of Irish immigrants, and, along with the parochial school, played a profound role in assimilating and Americanizing the sons and daughters of Erin.

The bombardment of Fort Sumter in Charleston Harbor by Confederate forces in the spring of 1861 incited what poet Walt Whitman called a "volcanic upheaval" from Maine to Minnesota as citizens gathered in county courthouses and town halls to volunteer to put down the rebellion. In an editorial, the *Boston Pilot*, the city's leading Catholic newspaper, patriotically exclaimed, "the Irish will build a wall of fire around the Union." Colonel Thomas Cass, a successful Boston Irish shipping merchant destined to give his life for his adopted country at Malvern Hill, organized the Massachusetts 9th Volunteer Regiment, an Irish unit, as it was proudly said, "from the Colonel to the drummer boy." The Ninth fought intrepidly in the Peninsular campaign and the ghastly battle of the Wilderness, winning the respect and admiration of their fellow Yankee soldiers.

In 1884, an alliance of Yankee and Irish Democrats elected Hugh O'Brien the first Irish-born Catholic mayor of Boston. Sometime in the next decade, the Irish surpassed the native Yankee stock in population, assuring the Celt's inevitable dominance of Boston's political future. In the opening decade of the 20th century, Patrick A. Collins and John F. Fitzgerald, or "Honey Fitz," as he was popularly called, were elected mayors, and the Irish became entrenched in the city's police and fire departments and in every strata of municipal government.

The Boston Irish community has produced many vivid personalities and leaders, including boxer John L. Sullivan, the ex-Fenain poet and editor John Boyle O'Reilly, ward boss Martin Lomasney, Mayor James Michael Curley, and William Henry Cardinal O'Connell, the redoubtable archbishop of Boston for almost four decades. On the eve of the Allied invasion of Normandy, Cardinal O'Connell succumbed to pneumonia at the age of 84 at his Italian Renaissance palace in Brighton—the outgoing, unassuming, South Boston-born Right Reverend Richard J. Cushing succeeding him as the sixth bishop of Boston. Representing a new generation of Boston Irish politicians, Maurice J. Tobin was elected mayor of Boston in 1937 and later governor of the Commonwealth.

In the years after World War II, Mayors John B. Hynes and John F. Collins brought new vigor and vision to city government, undertaking massive urban renewal projects. In Washington, Congressman John W. McCormack of South Boston was laboring and waiting to assume the Speakership of the U.S. House of Representatives. On election morning, November 8, 1960, Massachusetts' favorite son and Democratic Party presidential candidate John F. Kennedy cast his ballot at the polling booth in the abandoned West End branch of the Boston Public Library, and in the company of his wife, Jacqueline, boarded a plane for the short 25-minute flight to the Kennedy summer home in Hyannisport on Cape Cod to await the national will.

One

A Heritage of Misery

The Great Hunger of the 1840s, in which a million people perished, was a cataclysmic epic event in modern Irish history. This 1847 drawing by an artist named Smyth for the *Illustrated London News* shows a burial in Skibbereen, County Cork. Throughout the course of the famine, inhabitants of entire villages were buried "without coffin, without sermon, without anything that denoted respect for the dead."

An Irish family is evicted from their cabin, 1848. Some Irish landlords during the famine compassionately ignored overdue rents, provided food and clothing for their tenants, and sometimes subsidized passage to the United States and Canada. Others, anxious to convert their overcrowded estates into more profitable grazing lands for cattle and dairy farming and determined to reduce their poor relief tax, which was based upon occupied land, resorted to cold-hearted evictions. (*Illustrated London News.*)

Emigrants wait for passage on a quay, Cork Harbor, 1851. The long, exhausting journey to America often involved weeks of delay waiting for a ship to sail from an Irish port, forcing emigrants to seek shelter in overcrowded, unsanitary lodging houses. Naive about the world beyond their villages, Irish emigrants were easy prey for unscrupulous characters known as "land sharks," "harpies," and "man-catchers," representing disreputable passenger brokers and lodging houses. (*Illustrated London News*, 1851.)

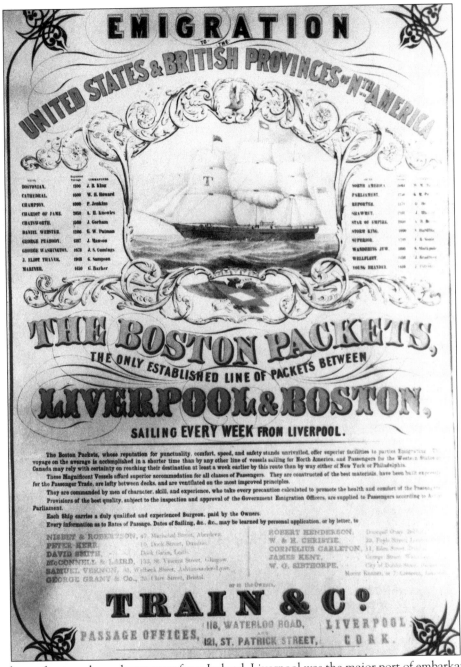

Twelve to fourteen hours by steamer from Ireland, Liverpool was the major port of embarkation for the bulk of Irish fleeing the famine. Vessels chartered under the American rather than British flag enjoyed a greater reputation for safety and cleanliness. This advertisement for the Boston Packets, owned by the Enoch Train Company, a pioneer in the passenger trade, guarantees prospective passengers prompt departures, spacious accommodations, and attention by a trained surgeon and a trained crew selected for "their character, skill, and experience" and who "take every precaution calculated to promote the health and comfort of the passengers." (Courtesy of the Bostonian Society.)

Boston goes about its business, c. 1854. On the eve of the Great Famine, Boston, a town described by one British diplomat as "the most English-like city in America," was a bustling, homogeneous Yankee Protestant community of around 114,000 inhabitants. (Courtesy of the Boston Athenaeum.)

An Irish family is reunited on Constitution Wharf, 1857. The woman dressed in American clothing on the right, with her arms lovingly outstretched, greets her aged mother, brothers, and a sister. Such heartwarming scenes, often shattered by "the wail from a broken heart," devastated by news of the death of a loved one, were repeated with the arrival of every emigrant ship to Boston. (*Ballou's Pictorial Drawing-Room Companion.*)

Located near Purchase and Oliver Streets, and within easy walking distance of Boston's waterfront, Fort Hill, an eminence of some 80 feet, was once a fashionable residential area inhabited by wealthy Yankee merchants and sea captains. Irish immigrants, however, displaced the retreating Yankees on Fort Hill and in the North and West Ends as handsome town houses and warehouses were converted into cheap tenements. (Courtesy of the Boston Public Library, Print Department.)

To cope with the large influx of sick and impoverished Irish immigrants, city officials established a quarantine station and temporary hospital on Deer Island, 5 miles out in Boston Harbor. In 1849 the mammoth Deer Island House of Industry, designed by architect Gridley J.F. Bryant and costing around $150,000, was built. Accommodating 1,500 inmates, the almshouse had a slate roof, eight circular water towers, workshops, a hospital, nursery, chapel, and "carriageway for receiving paupers." (Courtesy of the Boston Public Library, Print Department.)

The first Catholic church in Boston, the Cathedral of the Holy Cross on Franklin Place (now Franklin Street), was consecrated in 1803. Charles Bulfinch (1763–1844), who designed and supervised the construction of the church without charge, was presented with a silver tea urn by Boston's small pre-famine Catholic community as a token of their gratitude. President John Adams and other stout Puritans also donated funds to the construction of the church. A bell cast in Rome and imported from a Spanish monastery hung in the church's belfry. (Courtesy of the Archdiocese of Boston Archives.)

Born in Boston in 1812, the son of a prosperous Irish tailor and a graduate of the Boston Latin School, John Bernard Fitzpatrick (1812–1866) was appointed the third bishop of Boston in 1846. Only 33 years old at the time, Fitzpatrick oversaw a diocese that included Massachusetts, New Hampshire, Maine, and Vermont and worked tirelessly on behalf of Irish immigrants. Known to many as simply "Bishop John," Fitzpatrick in 1861 became the first Catholic prelate to receive an honorary degree from Harvard College. (Courtesy of the Archdiocese of Boston Archives.)

News of the Great Hunger in Ireland galvanized Boston's Yankee as well as its small Irish community. Sea captain and China trade merchant Robert Bennet Forbes (1804–1889) organized a crew and outfitted the *Jamestown*, a sloop of war moored at the Charlestown Navy Yard in 1847. A joint resolution of Congress put the *Jamestown* at his disposal to transport foodstuffs to a prostrate Ireland.

The *Jamestown* departs the Charlestown Navy Yard on March 28, 1847, an ensign emblazoned with a harp atop its main mast. The *Jamestown*, running deep with 800 tons of wheat, flour, potatoes, and clothing donated by the good people of New England, arrived 15 days later in the Harbor of Cork. Captain Forbes regarded the *Jamestown*'s mission as one of the most satisfying in his adventurous life. (Courtesy of the Boston Public Library, Print Department.)

Irish emigration to Boston and Massachusetts gave rise to the anti-immigrant Know-Nothing party, which captured the governor's office and virtually every seat in the Massachusetts General Court in 1854. In the political saddle, the Know-Nothings harassed Catholic schools with inspections, disbanded Irish militia companies, and tried to pass legislation mandating a 21-year wait before a naturalized citizen could vote. Peleg W. Chandler (1816–1889), a sterling Yankee Protestant, legal scholar, and immigration official, refused to acquiesce to the anti-immigrant hysteria of the Know-Nothings. In 1854 he roundly condemned, as inhumane and arbitrary, the deportation of helpless Irish immigrants "whose only fault is poverty and whose only heritage is misery." (Courtesy of the Society for the Preservation of New England Antiquities.)

Two
THY BROTHER'S KEEPER

Surrounded by decorations and dressed in their best clothes, youngsters at the Saint Vincent's Orphan Asylum on Camden Street in the South End gather for a special occasion, *c.* 1911. Dating back to the 1830s and under the direction of the Daughters of Charity, Saint Vincent's was the oldest Catholic charity in the city. (Courtesy of the Daughters of Charity Archives, Albany, New York.)

Sister Ann Alexis Shorb (1805–1875), the foundress and Lady Superior of St. Vincent's Orphan Asylum, was a "a woman of attractive personality, rare culture, great executive ability, and loved by both Catholics and Protestants." During the cholera epidemic that swept through the Irish slums of Boston in 1849, Sister Alexis and her co-workers brought food and medicine to the sick and prepared the dying for the Last Rites of the Church. Author Richard Henry Dana, a Protestant, was moved by such acts of Christian selflessness. In a letter to his intolerant wife, Sarah, he remarked, "In spite of all you say, I believe that if anyone goes to Heaven from Boston, it will be the Sisters of Charity and the Roman Catholic clergy." (Courtesy of the Archdiocese of Boston Archives.)

Imbued with a strong sense of stewardship toward the poor and unfortunate, Yankee physician and abolitionist Henry Ingersoll Bowditch (1808–1892) tended to the children at Saint Vincent's Orphan Asylum without compensation. He had the deepest admiration for Sister Ann Alexis, describing her as "one of my beau ideals of what an able, excellent Christian woman can do and become in this world." (Courtesy of the Carney Hospital, Dorchester.)

The children at Saint Vincent's ranged in age from 4 to 16. They received a general education, and to help them earn a living, the Sisters also taught the children how to cook, sew, and keep house. (Courtesy of the Daughters of Charity Archives, Albany, New York.)

Father George Foxcroft Haskins (1806–1872) founded the House of the Angel Guardian, an institution that provided shelter and education for street urchins, bootblacks, and "boys beyond parental control." An 1826 graduate of Harvard College and an Episcopalian priest, Haskins converted to Catholicism in 1840, studying for Holy Orders at Rome and Paris. Haskins's earlier ministry as a Protestant chaplain to inmates in public institutions and as pastor of a Catholic church in the immigrant North End gave him first-hand knowledge of neglected children, either abandoned by their parents or left to fend for themselves after their mothers and fathers died from ship's fever or cholera. In 1851, Haskins opened the House of the Angel Guardian in a modest dwelling in the North End. In addition to his charitable works, Haskins served as the first pastor of Saint Francis de Sales Church in Roxbury, and in 1859 he was elected the first Catholic member of the Boston School Committee. This exemplary priest left nearly all his estate to the Boston diocese, stipulating the proceeds be used for "the support of orphans and deserted boys." (Courtesy of the Archdiocese of Boston Archives.)

The House of the Angel Guardian's new quarters on Vernon Street in Roxbury was completed in 1860. Five floors in height, surmounted by a copula and a cross, the institution offered "ample and healthy" accommodations for 1,000 boys, ages 9 to 14. The discipline was "kind and paternal" and the fare "plain but abundant." Patrick C. Keely was the building's architect. (Courtesy of the Boston Athenaeum.)

The House of the Good Shepherd, incorporated in 1867, was situated in Roxbury on land once belonging to the Brigham estate. The institution, in the words of one of its annual reports, was a "refuge for penitent females." The Sisters of the Good Shepherd, a Catholic order with more than two centuries of experience in Europe working with troubled, wayward young women, were in charge of the institution.

In 1816, Andrew Carney (1794–1864) arrived in Boston from Ballanagh, County Cavan. A tailor by trade, he went into partnership with Jacob Sleeper, a devout Methodist and temperance advocate from Maine, and the firm profited handsomely by making U.S. army uniforms. Sage investments in real estate, insurance, and banking made Carney "the richest Catholic in New England" by 1845. Carney was "God's nobleman," noted a business associate, his generosity helping to build Boston College and the Immaculate Conception Church in the South End. In his will, Carney left money for the establishment of "a hospital where the sick without distinction of creed, color or nation shall be received and cared for." (Courtesy of the Carney Hospital.)

A Carney Hospital attendant stands alertly by his ambulance, *c.* 1904. An 1883 Boston guidebook maintained that no other hospital in New England had a more salubrious and breathtaking location than the Carney, established in 1863 on historic Dorchester Heights in South Boston. Convalescing patients could observe ships passing in and out of Boston Harbor, and cool sea breezes brought relief on sultry summer days.

The "Saint Mary's Infant Asylum and Lying-in-Hospital" was founded in Dorchester in 1874, the Daughters of Charity caring for foundlings and infants born out of wedlock, or in the expression of the day, to "unnatural parents."

Students attend a baking class at the Boston School for the Deaf c. 1911. At the turn of the century, Monsignor Thomas Magennis (1843–1912), the energetic pastor of Saint Thomas Aquinas Church in Jamaica Plain, was called to minister the Last Rites of the Church to a man who could neither speak nor hear. Dismayed by his inability to communicate with the dying man, Father Magennis went from pulpit to pulpit, raising money to establish the Boston School for the Deaf in his parish. (Courtesy of the Boston School for the Deaf.)

Seen in a triumphant moment in their lives, students receive their diplomas from the Boston School for the Deaf in 1916. In 1904, the Boston School for the Deaf, staffed by the Sisters of Saint Joseph, moved to a large suburban estate in Randolph, outside Boston. By 1907, the school had an enrollment of some 100 students. (Courtesy of the Boston School for the Deaf.)

Members of the Daughters of Charity, wearing their distinctive white cornettes, leave the Cathedral of the Holy Cross in 1932, following services commemorating the Order's 100th anniversary in Boston. Large numbers of young women from Irish families entered the religious life, devoting themselves to God and works of charity. Without them, the impressive network of charitable institutions and parochial schools, testifying to the self-reliance and pride of Boston's Irish community, would not have been feasible. (Courtesy of the Archdiocese of Boston Archives.)

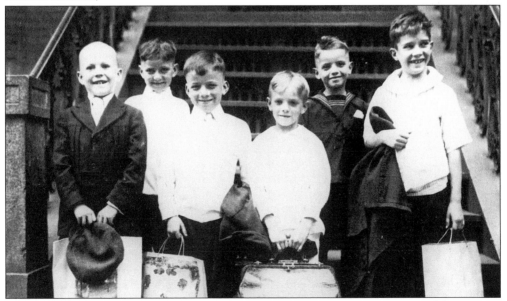

Their belongings in hand and faces glowing with excitement, youngsters set off for summer camp, sponsored by the Catholic Charitable Bureau *c.* 1921. (Courtesy of the Catholic Charitable Bureau, Boston.)

Intemperance was the great national vice of Ireland. In the late 1830s Father Theobald Mathew (1790–1856), "The Apostle of Temperance," began a moral revolution in Ireland, ministering the pledge to millions of his countrymen. Embraced enthusiastically by temperance advocates of every religious persuasion, Father Mathew received a hero's welcome in Boston in the summer of 1849, addressing throngs on the Boston Common and at Faneuil Hall. Father Mathew spent more than two years in the United States. He visited the White House and was voted a seat in the U.S. Senate, an honor conferred on only one other foreigner, the great Lafayette. Visible in this lithograph of Father Mathew is a banner bearing these words: "I promise to abstain from all intoxicating drinks, except used medicinally by order of a medical man and to discountenance the cause and practice of intemperance." (Courtesy of the Boston Athenaeum.)

Three

EARNING A LIVING

The wheelbarrow is the poor Irishman's country, a Yankee once remarked, as he toiled building America's canals, railroads, docks, and laying out Boston's streets and filling in the Back Bay. This 1871 photograph shows laborers leveling Fort Hill. (Courtesy of the Boston Public Library, Print Department.)

David Scannell (1796–1885) left his village in County Cork before the Great Hunger, settling in the North End around 1838. Like so many 19th-century Boston Irish immigrants, Scannell was listed in the *Boston City Directory* as simply a "laborer." Mr. Scannell died from injuries sustained in a fall from Lewis Wharf in 1885. He was 89. (Courtesy of Henry Scannell.)

The contracting business made Boston Irish families such as the Nawns, shown here standing next to their children in the wagon and surrounded by their teams of horses and workers attired in their Sunday finery, substantially wealthy. The Nawns helped build the Boston subway—the nation's first. (Courtesy of the Nawn family.)

Born in Londonderry, Ireland, contractor Charles Logue (1858–1919) was a member of Saint Peter's Parish in Dorchester and father of 13 children, 4 of whom entered the religious life. He was appointed Boston School House Commissioner by Mayor Patrick Collins in 1904. Logue collapsed and died while inspecting work on a church in December of 1919 and was eulogized by William Henry Cardinal O'Connell as a pious and honest man. Logue's "most conspicuous achievement" as a contractor, noted the *Boston Globe*, was the building of Fenway Park.

Pictured at the ground breaking ceremonies for Fenway Park, *c.* 1911, Logue is the bearded gentleman on the far right. (Courtesy of the Boston Public Library, Print Department.)

The residents of Boston were sustained by some 18 breweries in 1900, owned chiefly by Irish and German businessmen. Lawrence J. Logan (1842–1921), a Galway man, was president of the Boston Beer Company on D and Second Streets in South Boston. (Courtesy of the Boston Public Library, Print Department.)

The saloon of Mike McGreevey at 940 Columbus Avenue in Roxbury was within walking distance of the South End Grounds and Huntington Avenue Grounds, the homes of Boston's National and American League baseball teams in the early 1900s. A leader of the Royal Rooters, a band of baseball fanatics, McGreevey fitted his saloon, known as Third Base, with baseball-shaped light bulbs secured to the ceiling by ornaments resembling baseball bats. Note the spittoons. (Courtesy of the Boston Public Library, Print Department.)

John Donnelly (1830–1878) entered the bill poster trade in 1850, counting clipper ship owners who were urging Americans "To Go West" to California and P.T. Barnum, the showman and promoter, among his early clients. His sons carried on the enterprise of John Donnelly and Sons following his death in 1878, becoming by the turn of the century, one of the largest outdoor advertising companies in greater Boston. One of John Donnelly's descendants, Harvard-educated Edward Calvin Donnelly, married Governor James Michael Curley's daughter, Mary, in 1935, uniting two of Boston's most prominent Irish Catholic families. (Courtesy of Boston College, John J. Burns Library.)

The O'Keeffe grocery store was located at the corner of Dorchester Avenue and Charles Street. An immigrant from County Clare, Michael J. O'Keeffe (1866–1931) worked as a young grocery clerk in New York City before moving to Boston around 1895 and going into business for himself. Over the ensuing decades, O'Keeffe, possessing "a remarkable genius" for the grocery business, opened store after store. In 1925, O'Keeffe merged his "chain system of grocery stores" with two other provisions' giants, forming the famous First National Stores empire, which by the 1930s had more than 1,500 locations throughout New England.

Born in County Cavan, the venerable Patrick Donahoe (1811–1901), editor and publisher of the *Boston Pilot* and "Apostle of the Irish People in America," arrived in Boston at the age of ten with his widowed father in 1821. He entered the printing trade and in 1836 founded the *Boston Pilot*. The *Pilot*'s mission, Donahoe earnestly declared, was "the elevation of the Irish character in this country, the Independence of Ireland, and the overthrow of sectarian prejudice." An indefatigable worker and man of easy manner and charm, Donahoe steadily increased the *Pilot*'s circulation among the Irish in every corner of America, leading to the weekly being affectionately dubbed the "Irishman's Bible." The *Pilot*, along with ownership of the largest Catholic book publishing company in the country, a religious goods store, a foreign exchange, and passenger business, made Donahoe, who lived in a mansion opposite the Public Garden, "the richest and most influential Catholic layman in New England" by 1872. (Courtesy of the *Boston Pilot*.)

In July of 1868, Donahoe proudly featured this illustration of his elegant new establishment on the corner of Franklin and Frawley Streets on the front page of his *Pilot*. The seven-story building, designed by architect Gridley J.F. Bryant at the cost of $150,000, was "one of the most ornate and expressive examples of French renaissance architecture" and was "a monument to Irish-American enterprise," boasted the *Pilot*. It was built of white Concord marble and had a mansard roof, Luthern and French glass windows, and black walnut doors. (Courtesy of the *Boston Pilot*.)

The Great Boston Fire that roared through the central business district in November of 1872 consumed the Donahoe Block. Within a year's time, in a horrible streak of bad luck, Donahoe was burned out of two other locations. Forced into bankruptcy, the stouthearted Donahoe rebounded, starting a monthly magazine in 1878, and eventually repurchasing his beloved *Pilot*. He died the day after celebrating his 90th birthday in 1901. In 1908, the *Pilot* became the official newspaper of the archdiocese of Boston. (*Frank Leslie's Illustrated Newspaper.*)

Like so many other Irish immigrant women, Sarah Clancy Curley (1851–1921), the mother of Mayor James Michael Curley, worked as a domestic. According to one estimate, Boston domestics labored an average of 85 hours per week for just $4 in the 1880s. Heroic and uncomplaining, the Irish domestic, in an act of "unforgotten affection," frequently sent home a remittance to pay for the passage of other family members to Boston. (Courtesy of the Boston Public Library, Print Department.)

> WANTED—A good, reliable woman to take the care of a boy two years old, in a small family in Brookline. Good wages and a permanent situation given. No washing or ironing will be required, but good recommendations as to character and capacity demanded. Positively no Irish need apply. Call at 224 Washington street, corner of Summer street.
> bt   jy 2*

In 1868, the *Boston Transcript*, the favorite newspaper of Back Bay and Beacon Hill Yankee aristocrats, carried this "Help Wanted" advertisement for "a good, reliable woman" to care for a little boy in Brookline, emphatically noting, "Positively no Irish need apply."

The red-brick Saint Cecilia Church, dedicated in 1894 and located on the periphery of the Back Bay, was built by the faith and hard-earned wages of Irish domestics employed in the mansions lining Beacon Street and Commonwealth Avenue. Saint Cecilia's, with its predominately unmarried female congregation, was unlike any other church in Boston commented a writer in 1899. Few baptisms took place and in the summer months church attendance dwindled as servants accompanied their employers and families to the Berkshires or the seashore.

"A leader in his profession," physician William Aloysius Dunn (1852–1918) was a graduate of Boston College and Harvard Medical School. He had a thriving practice in the West End, served on the Boston School Committee in the 1880s and 1890s, and was an intimate of William Henry O'Connell, hiking through Italy and Switzerland with the future cardinal archbishop of Boston. (Courtesy of Francis A. Countway Library of Medicine.)

In 1873 Attorney Joseph D. Fallon (1837–1917), a native of Galway and graduate of Holy Cross College, was appointed the first Irish Catholic judge in Boston's history. A devoted family man, Judge Fallon was particularly stern with fathers who failed to support their children, wife beaters, and storekeepers who sold adulterated food and watered-down milk. (Courtesy of Holy Cross College Library.)

Born in County Roscommon and an 1859 graduate of Harvard Law School, Charles Francis Donnelly (1836–1909) is a heroic, neglected figure in Boston Irish history. An expert on canon law, Donnelly was the chief legal spokesman for the archdiocese of Boston during the difficult post–Civil War era. In 1888, during acrimonious hearings at the Massachusetts State House, Donnelly masterfully exposed and defeated legislative efforts to outlaw parochial schools under the guise of an educational reform bill.

The increasing demand for gas, electricity, and later, telephone service, provided steady employment for generations of Irish. This photograph was taken of gas workers in South Boston in 1894. (Courtesy of Special Collections, Boston College.)

In a city that attracted little manufacturing or heavy industry, unionizing efforts by Boston Irish labor leaders were confined mainly to the building trades, longshoremen, teamsters, brewery workers, and streetcar conductors. At a 1904 meeting of the Irish-dominated Boston Central Labor Union at Faneuil Hall, President Charles W. Eliot of Harvard University sits erectly at the center of the stage with his hands folded. (Courtesy of Harvard University Archives.)

Wearing his badge and his other symbol of civil authority, the billy club, Patrolman Joseph P. Clancy joined the Boston Police Department c.1880s. Once the preserve of Yankee Protestants, municipal positions went increasingly to the Irish as they grew in political strength. Seldom laid off, a policeman started at a respectable annual salary of $1,000 in 1887, and like the parish priest, was revered in the Irish neighborhood. (Courtesy of the Bostonian Society.)

The Irish by the turn of the century filled the ranks of the Boston Fire Department. Shown here outside the firehouse in 1888 are the gallant men of Ladder Company No. 1. The absence of a leg apparently did not deter the fireman in the front row, right, from carrying out his duties. (Courtesy of the Bostonian Society.)

William Doogue (1828–1906), the stubborn, strong-minded superintendent of the Boston Common and the Public Grounds from 1878 to 1906, was a native of Queen's County, Ireland. A florist by trade, Doogue helped transform the neglected, "odoriferous" Public Garden, mired in stagnant water from the Back Bay flats, into a 23-acre repose of botanical Victorian splendor.

Doogue regarded the Public Garden as a "pleasure grounds for the mass of God's people." Every spring and fall, under Doogue's tender care, the Public Garden radiated with brilliant flowers and exotic tropical plants. "In art gardening his advice is much sought and is always given, not only gratuitously, but with pleasure," noted a writer of Doogue in 1892. (Courtesy of the Society for the Preservation of New England Antiquities.)

Architect and Boston Buildings Department official Michael William FitzSimmons (1847–1913) was baptized at the old Cathedral on Franklin Place in 1847. He began his 35-year career as a civil servant in 1878, earning $1,250 a year as an Assistant Inspector of Buildings. By 1897, as Supervisor of Plans, he was making $2,500 annually. In 1900, FitzSimmons earned a measure of historical notoriety by refusing to grant his approval of "certain peculiarities" in the construction of Mrs. Isabella Stewart Gardner's palazzo on the Fenway. After some negotiations, work on the Fenway Court was allowed to proceed. A supporter of Home Rule for Ireland, FitzSimmons was a delegate to the National Convention of the United Irish League of America in Philadelphia in 1912. In a 1913 obituary, FitzSimmons was eulogized "as one of the most popular officials at City Hall." (Courtesy of Henry Scannell.)

Four

SCHOOLING

Students from SS Peter and Paul's Grammar School in South Boston pose for class photograph,
c. 1910. Along with teaching the three R's, the parochial school, or "Sisters' school," as it was
popularly called, preserved the Catholic faith and fostered patriotic American values. (Courtesy
of the Sisters of Saint Joseph Archives.)

Situated on Mount Benedict, a beautiful prospect in Charlestown, the Ursuline Convent opened in 1826, educating the children of prominent Catholic as well as Yankee Protestant families. On the night of August 11, 1834, a mob incited by medieval fantasies of convents as dens of sexual depravities and popish plots and also agitated by false tales of a student being held against her will, set fire to the convent. (Courtesy of the Boston Athenaeum.)

The ruins of the Ursuline Convent, with the hills of Somerville off in the distance stood as a stark reminder of religious bigotry until the Catholic church sold the land in 1875. (*Gleason's Pictorial Companion.*)

The eminent jurist Lemuel Shaw (1781–1861) presided over the trial of the 12 men indicted in the convent burning. All but one were acquitted. Reverend Benedict Joseph Fenwick (1782–1846), the Catholic bishop of Boston at the time of the destruction of the convent, joined by liberal Yankee Protestants, appalled that such an act of bigotry could take place within the shadow of Bunker Hill, birthplace of America's freedom, futilely petitioned the Massachusetts state legislature to indemnify the Catholic church on the grounds that its religion and civil liberties were violated.

Founded in 1854 and under the direction of the Sisters of Notre Dame de Namur, the Notre Dame Academy in Roxbury provided a genteel education to the daughters of well-to-do Irish Catholics and Yankee Protestants. Photographed here, fashionably dressed and radiating confidence and good breeding are the members of the Class of 1881. (Courtesy of the Sisters of Notre Dame Archives.)

In 1855, the Know-Nothing–controlled Massachusetts State legislature established a committee to inspect Catholic "Nunneries and Convents." They visited Holy Cross College in Worcester, a convent in Lowell, and Notre Dame Academy in Roxbury. At the latter institution, they went from the cellar to the attic, poking their bigoted noses into closets, and under beds and staircases, looking for evidence of a popish plot against the Republic, and upsetting both the nuns and students. Such outlandish behavior, satirized in this contemporary drawing entitled, "The 'Smelling Committee' Ferreting Out Romish Heresy," hastened the demise of the Know-Nothing party. (Courtesy of the Boston Athenaeum.)

Arriving in Boston in 1873, the Sisters of Saint Joseph educated generations of Irish Catholic students. Unlike some other religious orders, who either because of tradition or because of their congregation's constitution taught only girls, the Sisters of Saint Joseph instructed both sexes. In this photograph taken around 1947, the Sisters are attending the annual Lenten production of the popular play, *Pilot's Daughter*, at Mission Church's Saint Alphonus' Hall. (Courtesy of the Sisters of Notre Dame Archives.)

The overwhelming majority of 19th-century Irish Catholic students attended Boston's public schools, and some studied at the celebrated Public Latin School. In this photograph of an 1893 class at Latin School, students with Irish surnames such as Kelly and Scannell sit alongside Yankee blue bloods named Abbott, Sears, and Sprague. (Courtesy of Henry Scannell.)

Beginning with an enrollment of 12 students in the fall of 1843, the College of the Holy Cross, located on Mount St. James in Worcester, 40 miles from Boston and under the direction of the Jesuit Fathers, educated many of Boston's early Irish Catholic leaders. Bishop Benedict J. Fenwick, the bishop of Boston from 1825 to 1846 and the founder of Holy Cross, is buried on the school grounds "in the grave chosen and indicated by himself." (Courtesy of the Boston Athenaeum.)

Born in Georgia, the son of an Irish planter and former slave, Father James A. Healy (1830–1900) was a member of Holy Cross's first graduating class in 1849, delivering a dissertation on "the importance of moral principles as the only effective support of social order." Ordained at the Cathedral of Notre Dame in Paris in 1854, Healy was indispensable to Bishop John Bernard Fitzpatrick, serving as his secretary and as the first chancellor of the diocese. In 1875 Father Healy became bishop of Portland, Maine, making him the first black bishop in American Catholic church history. (Courtesy of Holy Cross College Library.)

Father John McElroy, the founder of Boston College, was born in Enniskillen, County Fermanagh, in 1782. He arrived on board a flax ship in Baltimore in 1803, soon entering the Jesuit novitiate at Georgetown College. From his college window, McElroy witnessed, "with all the pent-up hatred of an Irish rebel," wrote a biographer, the burning of the nation's capital by British soldiers during the War of 1812. Ordained in 1817, McElroy became a legendary preacher and missionary priest in Maryland and Virginia and served as a chaplain with General Zachary Taylor's army during the Mexican War. In 1847 McElroy became pastor of Saint Mary's Church in the immigrant North End. In the face of strong anti-Catholic, anti-immigrant prejudice, the gallant, unconquerable Jesuit finally procured land in 1857 for Boston College and the Church of the Immaculate Conception in the South End. A member of the Society of Jesus for 71 years, McElroy died at the age of 96 in Frederick, Maryland, in 1877. (Courtesy of University Archives, Boston College.)

Students and faculty are seated on the steps of Boston College, 1899. The college's "first pupils were of all shades of industry and idleness," remembered one wit. The Jesuit course of study—*Ratio Studiorum*—included classes in Latin, theology, philosophy, rhetoric, mathematics, church, and ancient history. "The moral and religious part of education is considered to be incomparably the most important," maintained the school's 1887 catalogue. Students thus were required to attend daily Mass, monthly confession, and annual spiritual retreats. (Courtesy of University Archives, Boston College.)

Holding a shovelful of soil and beaming with pride, Father Thomas Ignatius Gasson, the English-born president of Boston College, breaks ground for the construction of the school's first building on its new campus in beautiful Chestnut Hill in 1909. The location "seems almost intended by nature for the site of a large institution," noted the realty firm retained by the Jesuit Fathers to find a new home for their college. (Courtesy of University Archives, Boston College.)

Designed by the firm of Maginnis and Walsh and completed in 1913, the Recitation Building (later renamed Gasson Hall) at Boston College is one of the finest examples of English Collegiate Gothic architecture in the United States. Visible for miles around, its massive tower, housing four bells named in honor of Saint Ignatius of Loyola, founder of the Society of Jesus, and three other prominent Jesuits, is a "joy to the eye," observed the noted architect Ralph Adams Cram in 1921. (Courtesy of University Archives, Boston College.)

Maginnis and Walsh were preeminent in the field of 20th-century ecclesiastical architecture and were awarded by The American Institute of Architects two prestigious gold medals in the 1920s. Charles Donagh Maginnis (1867–1955), shown here, was born in Londonderry, Ireland, and Timothy Walsh (1868–1934), his associate for 34 years, was a native of Cambridge, Massachusetts, and brother of Reverend James Walsh, founder of the Maryknoll Missionary Fathers. In 1949, Maginnis was awarded an honorary degree by Harvard University.

49

Born in the West End, the son of a harness shop owner, William Stanislaus Murphy (1860–1916) graduated from Harvard College in 1885. He worked in the surveyor's office at the Boston Custom House, enjoying good health and life as a bachelor, "with no regrets," as he said in a letter to the class secretary. Murphy fulfilled what the school alumni magazine termed a "tribal wish" by bequeathing his estate of more than $50,000 to Harvard to assist any qualified student bearing his surname. (Courtesy of Harvard University Archives.)

The son of Boston Beer Company president, Lawrence J. Logan, Edward L. Logan (1875–1939) attended Boston Latin School and was an 1898 graduate of Harvard College and Harvard Law School in 1901. He represented South Boston in the state legislature, served as colonel with the famed Massachusetts Yankee Division in France during World War I, and was a Boston Municipal Court judge. Boston's international airport was named in Logan's honor. (Courtesy of Harvard University Archives.)

Prior to the chartering of "The Boston Ecclesiastical Seminary" in 1883, candidates for the Catholic priesthood studied in Rome, Paris, Montreal, or in seminaries beyond New England. Surrounded by rolling hills, trees, and ponds, Saint John's Seminary in Brighton, viewed here from Lake Street, *c.* 1890, was ideal for study and contemplation and was within easy proximity of Boston proper. Reverend John J. Williams, the archbishop of Boston, went personally to Paris to recruit the Sulpician Fathers to teach at his beloved seminary.

Beginning in 1925, seminarians at Saint John's enjoyed meals in the new refectory, a room, wrote a historian of the institution, "strikingly virile, in its dark oak panels and light gray acoustolith walls." Note the pulpit to the left below the crucifix. To cut down on expenses and to foster the virtue of humility, seminarians took turns serving meals. (Courtesy of the Archdiocese of Boston Archives.)

With Auxiliary Bishop Richard J. Cushing officiating, 30 seminarians received the Sacrament of Holy Orders at the Cathedral of the Holy Cross in the spring of 1941. (Courtesy of the *Boston Pilot*.)

Nursing school graduates of the Carney Hospital pose for this 1894 portrait. Where many of their immigrant mothers labored as domestic servants, seamstresses, factory workers or ran boarding houses, Irish-American women, beneficiaries of public and parochial school education, moved steadily into the nursing and teaching professions. (Courtesy of the Carney Hospital.)

The inspirational teacher, Anne Sullivan (1866–1937), right, is pictured with her prize student, Helen Keller (1880–1968). Sullivan was treated for eye problems at the Carney Hospital during the early 1880s when she was a young student at the nearby Perkins Institution for the Blind. Born in Agawam, Massachusetts, and nicknamed "Miss Spitfire" by the director of Perkins because of her strong-mindedness and undaunting spirit, Sullivan was valedictorian of her 1886 class. In her address Sullivan asserted, with wisdom far beyond her 19 years, "the advancement of society always has its commencement in the individual soul." (Courtesy of the Perkins School for the Blind.)

With their futures soon to be clouded by the Great Depression, students at Emmanuel College participate in Senior Class Day, 1929. Established in 1919 by the Sisters of Notre Dame and located in the fashionable Fenway, Emmanuel was the first Catholic women's college in New England. (Courtesy of Emmanuel College.)

Elizabeth O'Connell (1841–1921) arrived in Boston from Ireland as a young woman in 1860, working as a seamstress and dressmaker. In 1872, she married James O'Connell, a Corkman and mason, setting up house in Dorchester and rearing seven children. Mrs. O'Connell was ambitious for her offspring, insisting they all get a good education. Her first child, Joseph, born in 1872, attended Boston College and Harvard Law School and served in Congress. Her son John graduated from the Harvard Veterinary School in 1896, and James, Harvard College in 1902. Mrs. O'Connell's fourth son, Daniel, became a respected reporter and political editor for several Boston newspapers before graduating from Boston University Law School and joining his two brothers in the family law firm. In 1928, he was appointed to the Massachusetts Superior Court bench. Frederic, Mrs. O'Connell's youngest boy, attended Harvard College and was the baseball editor for the *Boston Post*, covering the first World Series in 1903. Elizabeth, the baby in the family, studied music and was a talented soprano. On Mrs. O'Connell's gravestone are inscribed the words: "Loving wife, devoted mother, who sacrificed greatly for education and advancement of her children . . ." (Courtesy of Lenahan O'Connell.)

Five

BIVOUACS
AND CAMPFIRES

Bowdoin-educated, Massachusetts governor John Albion Andrew (1818–1867), seated center, with his military staff, 1865, was one of President Lincoln's great "war governors." He was picturesquely described by one Boston Irishman as "a curly-haired, busy, spectacled, fat, little gentleman, reminding one of a high-pressure tug boat, with steam always up and continually huffing, paddling, and tugging at something." (Courtesy of the Boston Athenaeum.)

Dressed smartly in their blue-and-red uniforms and bearskin caps, the Columbian Artillery, chartered in 1798, and by the 1840s predominantly Irish, stand in formation outside their "gun house" in the North End, 1852. In 1855, with the anti-immigrant, Know-Nothing party controlling state government, the Columbian Artillery was forced to disband. It reorganized under a different guise and served as the nucleus for the famous Massachusetts Ninth Irish Volunteer Infantry Regiment during the Civil War. (*Gleason's Pictorial Companion*.)

Members of the Ninth stand outside their mess tent near the nation's capital in the early months of the war. The Ninth, before heading to the war front, trained on Long Island in Boston Harbor. On June 24, they marched in procession, escorted by Gilmore's Band, playing "all the popular airs of the Green Isle," to the State House on Beacon Hill. Presenting Colonel Thomas Cass with the state flag, Governor Andrew complimented the commander for raising "this splendid regiment." (Courtesy of the Library of Congress.)

Colonel Thomas Cass (1821–1862), organizer and commander of the Ninth Massachusetts Volunteer Irish Regiment, emigrated to America from Farmley, Queen's County, Ireland, as a five-month-old infant in 1821. He worked in his father's seaman's clothing shop in the North End, "married respectably," as one newspaper quaintly phrased it, and became a man of some means by engaging in the shipping trade to the Azores. Possessing "a decided taste for military life," Cass worked his way up the ranks of the Columbian Artillery. In responding to President Lincoln's request for troops, Cass firmly asserted, "Now is the time for me and my kind to show men who have been harping at us all our lives that the stars and stripes are as dear to us as to them." Cass died from wounds received at the battle of Malvern Hill in Virginia in July 1862. (Courtesy of the Library of Congress.)

Father Thomas Scully (1833–1902), an Irishman and newly ordained priest, served as chaplain of the Irish Ninth. He was taken prisoner by the Confederates while ministering to the wounded and dying at the battle of Gaines's Mill in Virginia in 1862, escaping when the sentry fell asleep at his post. Forced to resign because of ill health, Father Scully served as pastor of Saint Mary's Church in Cambridgeport for nearly four decades. A man of deep conviction, Scully, as noted by Yankee reformer Thomas Wentworth Higginson, was "afraid of nobody in the world except possibly the Pope." (Courtesy of the National Archives.)

Chaplain Scully and members of the Ninth assemble for Sunday morning Mass at Camp Cass, Arlington Heights, Virginia, 1861. (Courtesy of the Library of Congress.)

The Ninth suffered heavy casualties at Gaines's Mill and Malvern Hill during the Peninsular campaign in Virginia in the spring and summer of 1862. To replenish its ranks, the regiment issued this recruiting poster. It appealed to the martial ardor of the Irish race, offering both bounties and the consolation of "A Chaplain of The Old Faith." If disabled, a soldier and his family would be provided for with a "handsome" federal pension. "What employee," insisted the poster, "does the like?" (Courtesy of the Boston Public Library, Rare Books Department.)

The Glorious 9th!

IRISHMEN

To the Rescue!

Irish Americans of Massachusetts!

The indomitable valor and bravery which distinguished your ancestors on many a bloody battle-field in past ages, have descended to you untarnished. Your fellow countrymen of the 9th Massachusetts Regiment have proved at "Hanover Court House," at "Mechanicsville," at "Gaines' Mill," and at "Newtonville," that it has not degenerated. They are worthy inheritors of the courage and prowess of the heroes who fought at "Clontarf," at "Beal-an-ath-Buidhe," at "Limerick," at "Landen," at "Cremona" and "Fontenoy."

The Union and future glory of this great sanctuary of freedom is in danger. A host of Southern traitors seek to destroy our free democratic government, and erect upon its ruins a contemptible and Despotic Aristocracy.

Irish valor and bravery, have, to a great extent, thus far, impeded the march of these native Vandals, and driven back their superior numbers in dismay. Wherever the "chivalry" of the South have dared to encounter, on an open field, our Irish braves, they have found to their cost that Irishmen, as of old, are still invincible.

No Regiment in the service of the United States, has earned more imperishable glory than the 9th Regiment Massachusetts Volunteers, and its late gallant and heroic Colonel. The fortunes of war have thinned its ranks; it must not be allowed to perish for want of brave men to fill up its numbers.— The honors it has earned you can share. The living heroes of the 9th are still "eager for the fray." They pant to be led once more against the enemy—the enemy of human freedom—the enemy of mankind. They long to avenge their brave compatriots.

"We are to revenge them!—no joy shall be tasted. / The harp shall be silent, the maiden unwed.

Our halls shall be mute, and our fields shall be wasted. / Till vengeance is wreaked on the libertieldes' head."

They call upon you from the banks of the James to fill up their ranks, to share with them the laurels of the past and the glory of the future. Will you not respond to their call?

"Our green flag flutters o'er us, / The friends we've tried are by our side / And the foe we hate, before us."

The City of Boston has voted a

Bounty of $100!

In addition to thirty-eight dollars allowed by the United States, for every volunteer who joins the 9th Regiment, to defend the best and freest government ever vouchsafed to man. In joining the Ninth, you join your own gallant kith and kin. You will be led to the battle-field by officers of your own ancient race, who have proved themselves inferior to no others of our grand army. Here, too, the

FLAG OF IRELAND!

Is carried side by side with the Starry Banner, and Irish bravery will obtain the credit it deserves. The laurels you win will deck your own brows—others will not obtain the credit which belongs to you. And while your prowess and invincible valor shed additional lustre on

The Stars and Stripes!

They will cast a bright ray of glory on the

GREEN FLAG!

and the unconquerable nationality it represents.

In this Regiment you will have

A CHAPLAIN OF THE OLD FAITH

To minister to your spiritual wants and dispense the priceless blessings of religion.

Your families will be provided for by the BOUNTY OF THE STATE, and you will receive in Pay, Rations and Clothing, an allowance more than that for which many of you toil at laborious drudgery, equally, if not more dangerous, than the field of honor and glory.

The nation provides also a handsome pension for you if disabled, and for your wives and little ones if you fall at the post of duty. What employer, let us ask, does the like?

Our brave countrymen, hitherto, have rushed to the battle-field without bounty, with little hope of reward. Can YOU hesitate NOW, when such ample provision is made for you and yours?

Let the ranks of the glorious 9th be at once manned by heroes, worthy successors of those who have fallen, and fit companions of the veterans still eager for the fight. This Regiment is yours. Its history—its glory—its past—its future, are yours, and shed a lustre not on you only, but on the Irish race. The only power in Europe which supports the South is your ancient enemy, the Government of England.

"Then onward your green banners rearing; / Go flesh every sword to the hilt;

On our side is virtue and Erin, / On theirs is the Saxon and guilt."

The Sum of $188,00

Will be paid to each volunteer as soon as mustered into service. Pay and Rations from enlistment.

Transportation for volunteers, over any of the railroads to Boston, furnished to those wishing to join.

The undersigned has received full power from the City Government of Boston to recruit the ranks of the 9th REGIMENT to its full quota.

All applications for enlistment to be made at the

Headquarters, 112 Washington Street, Boston,

Over Little & Brown's Bookstore, to

Capt. B. S. TREANOR,

OR HIS AUTHORIZED AGENTS.

J. E. Farwell & Co., Steam Job Printers, 37 Congress Street, Boston.

General Thomas Francis Meagher (1823–1867), born in County Wexford and son of a wealthy merchant, was banned to Tasmania in 1849 for plotting sedition against England. Escaping, he rose to prominence in New York City as a journalist, lecturer, and politician. He was a handsome, dashing figure, "with a wonderful flow of language and poetic ideas," remembered a fellow soldier. Meagher, as a member of a New York volunteer regiment, had his horse shot from underneath him at the first battle of Bull Run. He soon formed the Irish Brigade that fought valiantly at the battle of Antietam and was virtually annihilated at the battle of Fredericksburg in 1862. General Meagher visited Boston on several occasions, delighting an audience at the Tremont Temple in 1864 with an account of his escape from Tasmania and of how the men of the Army of the Potomac observed Saint Patrick's Day. A year later, Meagher was appointed territorial secretary of Montana. On a summer night in 1867, Meagher fell from a steamer on the Missouri River, his body never being recovered. He was only 43. (Courtesy of the National Archives.)

In January of 1862, the front page of the *Boston Pilot* featured this rousing illustration of a soldier carrying the colors of the newly formed Massachusetts 28th Volunteer Regiment. Embroidered on the Regiment's flag were shamrocks; an Irish wolfhound; an American eagle; a harp, the national symbol of Erin; the words, "Fostered under thy wing we will die in thy defense"; and the ancient Gaelic battle cry: "FAG AN BEALAC, " meaning "clear the road." In December of 1862, the 28th Regiment, as part of General Meagher's Irish Brigade, won an enduring place in American military history with its heroic, futile assault, in the face of murderous Confederate musket and battery fire, of Marye's Heights at Fredericksburg. (Courtesy of the *Boston Pilot*.)

Handsome and resolute-looking, Colonel Patrick R. Guiney (1835–1877) succeeded the mortally wounded Colonel Cass as commander of the Irish Ninth in July of 1862. A Tipperary man, Guiney worked as a wheel-boy in a rope factory, attended Holy Cross College, and was a lawyer by profession. (Courtesy of Holy Cross College Library.)

Guiney was struck in the face by a sharpshooter's bullet at the battle of the Wilderness in 1864, losing his left eye. His daughter Louise recalled the childhood horror of seeing her disfigured father, whom she idolized, standing at the door of their home, pathetically awaiting recognition. Louise Guiney wrote the following: "What was this spectre, with whom I must not frolic, on whose shoulders I must not perch, whose head, bound in bandages, I must not handle?" (Courtesy of Holy Cross College Library.)

Patrick Sarsfield Gilmore (1829–1892) was the greatest bandmaster and concert promoter of his day and composer of the Civil War classic, "When Johnny Comes Marching Home." A native of Galway and musical prodigy, Gilmore arrived in Boston around 1849, and following an apprenticeship with several ensembles, formed his own celebrated "Gilmore's Band." During the Civil War, Governor Andrew appointed Gilmore "Bandmaster-General and Chief Musician," a position tasking the debonair Irishman with recruiting and training musicians for the Bay State's regimental bands. (Courtesy of Michael J. Cummings.)

To mark the restoration of peace between the North and South, Gilmore persuaded Boston's "money men" in 1869 to construct a 50,000-seat coliseum, near present-day Copley Square, for a National Peace Jubilee. Hailed by *Harper's Weekly* as "the grandest musical enterprise the world has ever witnessed," the five-day musical extravaganza drew thousands of spectators, including President Ulysses S. Grant, believed to be the man tipping his tall hat in the carriage, forefront. (Courtesy of the Boston Public Library, Print Department.)

Sligo-born sculptor Martin Milmore (1844–1883) fashioned portrait busts of Longfellow, Emerson, Wendell Phillips, and other New England luminaries, and his soul-inspiring statues and monuments to the Union dead served as models for a generation of sculptors. "Milmore was a picturesque figure," declared his friend, sculptor Daniel Chester French. He was tall and had large dark eyes and long dark hair that drooped over his neck. Like many artists of his day, Milmore wore a broad-brimmed black hat and a cloak. "His appearance was striking, and he knew it," said French. (*Frank Leslie's Illustrated Newspaper.*)

Martin Milmore's arresting bronze *Citizen Soldier*, or *Roxbury Soldiers Monument*, at Forest Hills Cemetery in Jamaica Plain was dedicated on Memorial Day, 1868. The work, described by one critic as "a notable landmark in the history of American art," launched Milmore's career as the great commemorator of the Union dead. (Photograph by Greg Cecconi.)

Assisted as he was on many of his other undertakings by his older brother Joseph, a talented stonecutter, Milmore completed the American *Sphinx* for Mount Auburn Cemetery in Cambridge in 1872. The work, honoring the Union dead, was commissioned by Jacob Bigelow (1787–1879), the famous botanist, Harvard physician, and founder of Mount Auburn in 1831. Bigelow prevailed upon Milmore to use the figure of the sphinx, which has its roots in ancient Greek and Roman mythology and symbolizes beauty, strength, duration, and intellect. (*Frank Leslie's Illustrated Newspaper.*)

The great *Sphinx*, cut from a single block of Hallowell, Maine granite in a shed across the street from Mount Auburn, is transported to its permanent location. Eighty-five and blinded by cataracts, Doctor Bigelow, according to one account, "had to be lifted to trace with his fingers the enigmatic countenance" of the *Sphinx*. Some lot owners found the *Sphinx* disconcerting, complaining to the cemetery trustees that it might "occasion fright to horses." (Courtesy of the Boston Public Library, Fine Arts Department.)

Milmore's *Soldiers' and Sailors' Monument*, located on Flagstaff Hill on the Boston Common, was dedicated on September 17, 1877. Milmore spent five years in Rome working on the heroic-size statues and intricate bronze bas-reliefs that adorn the monument. On the projecting corners of the monument's pedestal are four 8-foot bronze figures: a soldier wearing a cap and an overcoat and holding a musket; a sailor leaning on a cutlass and looking seaward; a seated female figure, the *Muse of History*, dressed in Greek robes, holding a stylus and tablet; and another female figure, *Peace*, grasping an olive branch. An 11-foot bronze statue of the *Genius of America* crowns the 70-foot monument. In her left hand, she holds a banner of the Republic, and in the other, a sheathed sword and wreaths of laurel. Milmore has her facing to the South, in a spirit of reconciliation. A parade, reviewed by President Rutherford B. Hayes and numbering 20,000 marchers, many of them veterans of the Grand Army of the Republic, preceded the dedication of the monument. Only 39 years old, unmarried, and at the peak of his artistic powers, Milmore died in 1883. Wendell Phillips, Patrick Donahoe, and Thomas Ball, Boston's leading sculptor and in whose studio Milmore worked as a boy, tending to the fires and sweeping floors in return for use of clay, a mallet and chisel, served as pallbearers at his funeral.

Six

FAITH AND FAMILY

Archbishop John J. Williams (1822–1907) sits front row, center, with the directors of Holyhood Cemetery in suburban Brookline, c. 1900. Born in Boston in 1822 and the son of a blacksmith from Tipperary, Williams succeeded his deceased mentor and friend John Bernard Fitzpatrick in 1866 as bishop of Boston. Tall and strikingly handsome in his prime, Williams was a prudent administrator, revered by his flock and fellow priests, and was diplomatic in his relations with Yankee Boston. (Courtesy of the Archdiocese of Boston Archives.)

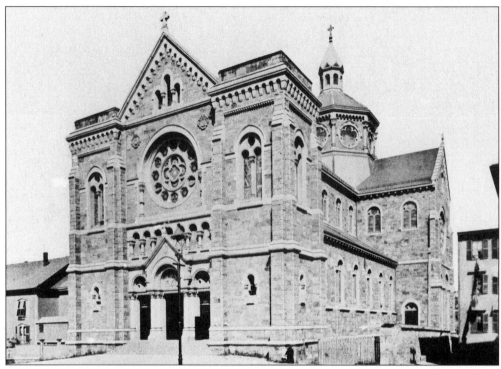

Situated on the slopes of Parker Hill, Roxbury, and under the direction of the esteemed preaching order, the Redemptorists' Fathers, Our Lady of Perpetual Help Church, or Mission Church as it was popularly called, was dedicated in 1878. William Shickel, a German-born New York architect, "aided by good and honest mechanics," built this splendid edifice for little more than $200,000. The shrine of the church became famous for the miraculous cures attributed to it.

In 1910, two magnificent bell towers, crowned by 9-foot-high crosses, were added to Mission Church. The Parochial Residence, to the left, was built in 1902. It contained a grand community chapel and an exquisite library, with galleries, spiral staircases, and thousands of volumes. The Redemptorists' Fathers lived in individual rooms, described in a parish history as "fairly large, airy, and lightsome, but furnished with ascetical severity." (Courtesy of the Boston Public Library, Print Department.)

The Mission Church Parish was a burgeoning, vibrant parish of more than 9,000 worshippers by 1890. The parish sponsored all kinds of sodalities, fraternities, and athletic teams to keep youngsters occupied and to ward off "evil influences." In 1901 the Mission Church Field Band was formed. Outfitted in natty, braided, blue coats and white trousers, the band was popular at parish field days and civic events. (Courtesy of Mission Church Parish.)

Standing beside a banner bearing the inscription, "Blessed Holy Name Jesus," priests and laymen from Mission Church mark a religious observance, c. 1900. (Courtesy of Mission Church Parish.)

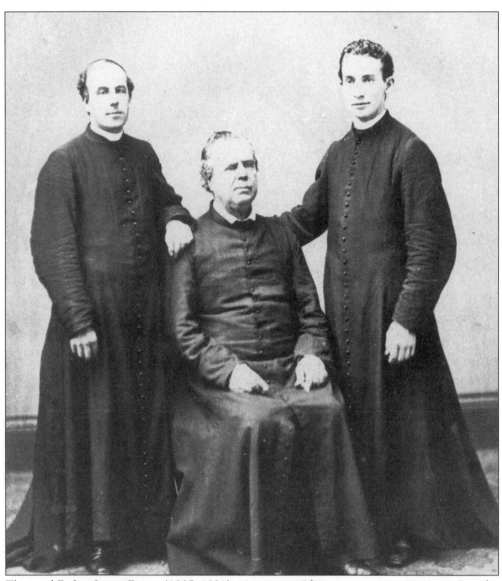

The aged Father James Fitton (1805–1881), center, was "the greatest missionary priest" in the history of Catholic New England. Born in Boston in 1805, the son of a wheelwright from Lancashire, England, Fitton was ordained in 1827 by Bishop Benedict J. Fenwick at the Cathedral on Franklin Place. The Boston diocese at the time Fitton commenced his missionary career embraced all six New England states. Of rugged, indomitable spirit, Fitton ministered to Irish immigrants laboring on canals, railroads, and in remote factory villages from Bridgeport to Hartford, to Springfield, Worcester, Providence, and throughout the Berkshires and Vermont, contracting rheumatism from sleeping in damp church basements. In the 1830s Fitton established an academy in Worcester, later conveying the school's 52 acres to Bishop Fenwick for the founding of the College of the Holy Cross. In the last two decades of his life, Fitton was also active in the temperance movement, translated devotional tracts, and established four parishes in water-surrounded East Boston, his "island diocese." The diocese's oldest priest, Father Fitton delivered the main sermon at the dedication of the Mission Church in 1878. (Courtesy of the Sisters of Notre Dame Archives.)

Built of New Hampshire white granite, the Church of the Immaculate Conception, designed by Patrick C. Keely and located on Harrison Avenue in the South End, was dedicated in 1861. Philosopher George Santayana attended Sunday Mass at the Jesuit-run Immaculate Conception as a young man in the 1880s, recalling in his memoirs some 60-odd years later, one Father Jeremiah O'Connor, "a young and very oratorical Irishman, eloquently proclaiming Catholic Truth against all heresies." (Courtesy of the Boston Public Library, Print Department.)

The interior of the Immaculate Conception Church, design by Arthur D. Gilman, is "as magnificent as the exterior," remarked a visitor in the 1890s. "White in color, lofty in sweep, graceful and chaste in lines, the effect produced on the beholder can be nothing but that of religious awe and admiration," he asserted. (Courtesy of the Boston Public Library, Print Department.)

Several venerable Boston Protestant meetinghouses and churches, their pews abandoned by parishioners fleeing the hordes of Irish immigrants invading their neighborhoods, were acquired by the Catholic clergy to meet the pressing needs for places of worship. In 1862 the Twelfth Congregational Church on Chambers Street in the West End was purchased for $27,000 and consecrated as Saint Joseph's Church. The pillared, brick structure had plain glass windows, galleries, and a "large melodious organ."

The New North Church, designed by Charles Bulfinch in 1804 and located on Hanover Street in the North End, was the center of Unitarianism in Boston for generations, Reverend Francis Parkman, the father of the illustrious historian, serving as pastor from 1813 to 1849. Isolated by the immigrant flood, the structure was sold to the Catholic church in 1862 and consecrated as Saint Stephen's. Hanging in the tower of the church is a bell made by Paul Revere.

The Church of Saint Vincent de Paul, on E and West Third Streets, South Boston, has a fascinating and resilient past. In 1848 Bishop John Bernard Fitzpatrick purchased an old Quincy granite Unitarian meetinghouse on Fort Hill, swarming with new Irish immigrants, and consecrated it as Saint Vincent's Church. Immediately after the Civil War, Fort Hill was leveled, forcing Saint Vincent's to close. Granite blocks taken from the old church on Fort Hill were transported to South Boston and used to form the eastern and southern walls of the new Saint Vincent's, dedicated in 1874.

Designed by Gridley J.F. Bryant and dedicated in 1845, SS Peter and Paul's Church in South Boston, seen here in 1892, was ravaged by fire three years later, leaving only "the bare walls and a pile of smoking ruins." Rededicated on Thanksgiving Day, 1853, the church was "more spacious and beautiful than ever before," reported the *Boston Pilot*. Patrick Keely, "the whole-souled Christian artist," designed the interior and over the main entrance rose an imposing tower and steeple.

In 1872, Father Peter Ronan (1844–1917), a native of County Westmeath, founded Saint Peter's Parish in the rural Protestant stronghold of Dorchester. Genial, persevering, and blessed "with unusual common sense," Father Ronan during his 45-year tenure as pastor built a splendid church, parochial school, convent, and rectory. By the early 1900s, Saint Peter's Parish, home to many triple-deckers, had 6,000 families and was the largest parish in the archdiocese. (Courtesy of Saint Peter's Parish.)

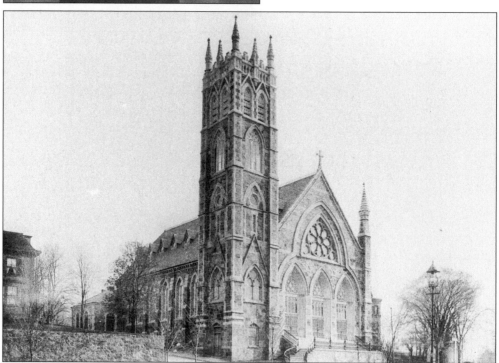

Poised graciously on Meeting House Hill and its 150-foot grand Norman tower, completed in 1891, dominating the Dorchester landscape, Saint Peter's Church was designed by the eminent Irish-born architect Patrick C. Keely. Like so many dedicated immigrant priests of his generation, Father Ronan, along with attending to his priestly duties, supervised the daily construction of his church, frequently climbing the scaffolding to inspect the progress of the workmen.

Father Ronan appears with organizers of the parish's first lawn party, *c.* 1890. During the pioneer days of Saint Peter's, Father Ronan was aided by his saintly mother, Margaret Ronan, who resided with her priestly son, doing the cooking, washing, and housekeeping. Mrs. Ronan, who had another son who was a priest, died in 1888. Saint Margaret's Hospital, which Father Ronan help found in Dorchester in 1911, was named after his mother's patron saint.

Father Ronan, mounted on camel, center, poses for the camera within the shadows of the pyramids during a pilgrimage to the Holy Land around 1898. (Courtesy of Saint Peter's Parish.)

Patrick C. Keely (1816–1896), a native of Kilkenny, was the pioneer Catholic church architect of 19th-century America, designing an estimated 600 to 700 churches, including a dozen or more in Boston. Keely maintained that for an individual to succeed as an architect, one had to be honest, frugal, and knowledgeable of his craft. A resident of Brooklyn, Keely attended Mass daily and was the father of 17 children.

In the 1870s, Patrick Keely designed Holy Trinity Church on Shawmut Avenue in the South End for Boston's "German-speaking Catholics." The interior of Holy Trinity was "as perfect a specimen of the early German Gothic as it is possible to reproduce," the *Boston Pilot* glowingly reported. The church was "fitted with handsome pews of chestnut," stained-glass windows, and carved wood statues of the apostles imported from Aix-La-Chapelle, with Saint Matthias taking the place of the fallen Judas.

No longer adequate, the historic old Cathedral on Franklin Place was closed in 1860. After years of delay because of the Civil War, workmen finally began building the new Cathedral of the Holy Cross in the South End in 1867. As evidenced in this lithograph by J.H. Buffords, Patrick Keely envisioned building an edifice on the scale and grandeur of the great European cathedrals, with spires soaring 200 and 300 feet to the heavens. Financial restraints and an eagerness to put the Cathedral into service, however, forced the abandonment of the spires. Described by one contemporary newspaper as "the grandest religious event for the Catholics of this generation," the dedication of the Cathedral took place on December 8, 1875. Built primarily of Roxbury puddingstone and costing $1.5 million, the Cathedral accommodated 3,500 worshippers, making it the largest church in New England. Bricks retrieved from the Ursuline Convent, destroyed a generation earlier by a mob, form the arch over the entrance to the nave. Bishop Fitzpatrick and Archbishop Williams are also interred in crypts at the Cathedral. (Courtesy of the Archdiocese of Boston Archives.)

The Cathedral, with its capped towers and elegant rose window, appears here soon after the construction in 1902 of the Boston Elevated, its rumbling trains drowning out sermons and choirs for generations. (Courtesy of the Boston Public Library, Print Department.)

Looking from the main alter toward the entrance and choir gallery, this view shows the majestic interior of the Cathedral. The Cathedral's organ, one of the largest in the United States, has more than 5,000 pipes and is "of unsurpassed purity of tone and remarkable power," noted an 1880s Boston guidebook. (Courtesy of the Boston Public Library, Print Department.)

"Set back from the street, and bold in outline," Saint Columbkille's, located in the Brighton district of Boston, "must be ranked as one of the finest churches in the city," pronounced a writer in 1899. Its cornerstone was blessed in 1872, the famous Irish Dominican, Father Thomas Burke, delivering the sermon. The lower church was completed in 1875, and after overcoming financial obstacles, the upper church was opened for public worship on July 4, 1880.

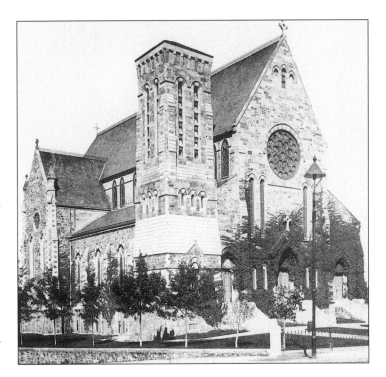

The cornerstone for the Gate of Heaven Church in South Boston was laid in 1896. The work of George A. Clough, the Gate of Heaven is a splendid example of 13th-century French Gothic–style architecture. "Its great height and comparative shortness, its rounded apse and small projections at the transepts, all stamped it with this distinctive character, and the effect is compact, soaring and strenuous," contended one writer. (Courtesy of the Boston Public Library, Print Department.)

Captured in this stunning portrait, taken around 1904, are four generations of the Rogers family. Mary Dunn Rogers (1813–1905), right, who arrived in Boston around the time of the Great Famine, was married to Patrick Henry Rogers, a native of County Louth, a member of the Roxbury Common Council in the 1850s and 1860s, and a builder by trade. Standing is Mrs. Rogers's daughter, Ann Rogers Faunce (1846–1934). To Mrs. Rogers's left are her granddaughter Louise Faunce Roach (1872–1928) and great-granddaughter Estelle (1904–). (Courtesy of Henry Scannell.)

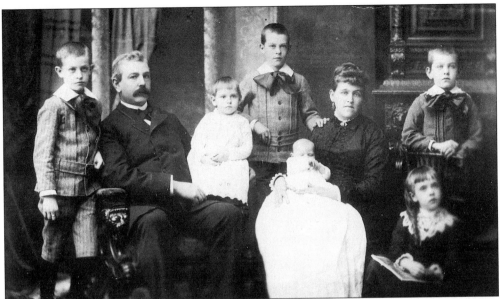

The family of Abraham T. Rogers, son of Patrick Henry Rogers and Mary Dunn Rogers, sits decorously for a photographer, c. 1880s. Abraham Rogers's little girl, Mary, or Mollie, as she was affectionately called, front, right, graduated from Smith College in 1905 and taught zoology at the Northampton, Massachusetts school for six years. Inspired by the young Protestant women from Smith, who went to China as missionaries, and the work of Maryknoll priest Father James Walsh, Mollie Rogers founded the Catholic Missionary Congregation of the Maryknoll Sisters in 1912. (Courtesy of the Maryknoll Mission Archives, Maryknoll, New York.)

The Rogers clan gathers for a Thanksgiving Day in 1907. (Courtesy of Henry Scannell.)

A parish baseball team in East Boston posed for this *c.* 1900 photograph. The tall, lean, young man standing next to the priest with the mitt is Joseph P. Kennedy, father of President John F. Kennedy. (Courtesy of the John F. Kennedy Library.)

Harvard College denied James Brendan Connolly of South Boston a leave of absence to compete in the first modern Olympic Games in Athens, Greece, in 1896. Freshman Connolly, pictured front row, left, in this 1897 Knights of Columbus track meet in Roxbury, participated anyway, finishing first in the "Hop, Step, and Jump" event.

Seven

THE POLITICAL
ASCENDANCY OF THE
IRISH

Boston's new City Hall, facing School Street, was designed by Gridley J.F. Bryant and Arthur D. Gilman and was dedicated on September 18, 1865, by Mayor Frederic W. Lincoln Jr. It was built of granite quarried from the famous Rattlesnake Ledge in Concord, New Hampshire, and cost a half-million dollars to complete. (Courtesy of the Boston Public Library, Print Department.)

Crowned by a Louvre-style dome and a guilded eagle, Boston City Hall housed the various departments and divisions of municipal government. A mayor and a bicameral legislature governed Boston during the decades after the Civil War. The mayor's office, or Room Number One, as it was sometimes called, was located on the second floor, far right. The chamber of the city's upper legislative body, the 12-member Board of Aldermen, was also on the second floor. The unwieldy Common Council, consisting of 75 members, 3 from each of the city's 25 wards, deliberated on the third floor. Up until 1895, the term of office for the mayor was one year. It was then extended to two years, and with the adoption of a new city charter in 1909, it was increased to four years. (Courtesy of the Boston Public Library, Print Department.)

Hugh O'Brien (1827–1895), the first Irish-born Catholic mayor of Boston, came to the Hub as a little boy in 1832. He was the successful printer and publisher of a shipping journal, president of the Charitable Irish Society of Boston and a savings bank, and director of a Catholic orphanage. A resident of Roxbury and a Democrat, O'Brien was elected to the Board of Aldermen in 1875 and in 1884 defeated Republican incumbent Augustus Pearl Martin for mayor. O'Brien was elected to four consecutive one-year terms as mayor. A man of foresight, O'Brien championed the acquisition of parklands, which under the guiding genius of landscape architect Frederick Law Olmsted, became the city's spectacular "Emerald Necklace." In 1888, he laid the cornerstone for the magnificent public library at Copley Square. On August 1, 1895, O'Brien suffered a fatal heart attack at the parochial residence of his son, Father James J. O'Brien, pastor of Saint Catherine's Parish in Somerville. O'Brien was eulogized as a man of "virtue and forbearance," a friend of the "colored citizens" of Boston, and for leaving to posterity "the grandest system of public parks in the world." (Courtesy of the Bostonian Society.)

"He stands a conspicuous example of what a fine graft can be made of Irish and American stock," asserted a writer of Patrick A. Collins (1844–1905) in 1890. A refugee from the Great Famine, Collins worked as an upholsterer, graduated from Harvard Law School in 1871, and served in the state legislature and three terms in Congress. In 1892, President Grover Cleveland appointed Collins consul-general to London. In 1901, he was overwhelmingly elected to his first term as mayor of Boston. (Courtesy of Special Collections, Boston College.)

Patrick Collins worked as an office boy for attorney Robert Morris (1823–1882), the first black man to be admitted to the Boston Bar. Morris had so many Irish immigrants as clients that he was often referred to as the "Irish lawyer." A convert to Catholicism, Morris was buried with great solemnity from the Immaculate Conception Church in the South End in 1882. Collins served as one of the pallbearers. (Courtesy of the Social Law Library, Boston.)

In 1888, Congressman Collins moved from his residence on East Fourth Street in South Boston to this stately mansion atop Mount Ida near Saint Peter's Church in Dorchester. Five years later Collins put the house up for sale, informing his private secretary he would be content to receive $30,000 for it. (Courtesy of the Society for the Preservation of New England Antiquities.)

Mayor Collins, holding a walking cane, stands with the great orator, and three-time Democratic presidential nominee, William Jennings Bryan, c. 1900. Collins died 16 months into his second term as mayor on September 14, 1905. A monument erected to Collins in 1908 and located on Commonwealth Avenue in the heart of the Back Bay bears the legend, "A talented, honest, generous, serviceable man." (Courtesy of Special Collections, Boston College.)

Patrick Joseph Kennedy (1858–1929), paternal grandfather of President John F. Kennedy, was a prosperous saloonkeeper, liquor import dealer, and ward boss of East Boston, serving in the state legislature. The saloon served as a place for Irish immigrants to congregate, exchange news about the old country, and to talk politics. Irish saloonkeepers and liquor dealers dominated Boston's Democratic Ward Committee, assailed by temperance and civil service reformers as "The Grog Shop Committee." (Courtesy of the Boston Public Library, Print Department.)

With legs outstretched and surrounded by all the comforts of turn-of-the-century, middle-class respectability, P.J. Kennedy ponders his hand in a card game. (Courtesy of the John F. Kennedy Library.)

88

An 1893 graduate of Boston College, where he captained the school's first football team, and a graduate of Harvard Law School, Joseph F. O'Connell (1872–1942) of Dorchester served in the U.S. Congress from 1907 to 1911. O'Connell's commanding personality and attributes were succinctly summarized in his campaign slogan, "Able, Active, Aggressive." (Courtesy of Lenahan O'Connell.)

Congressman O'Connell, back row, far right, poses with members of the Democratic congressional baseball team, Washington, D.C., 1910. Congressman James M. Cox of Ohio, front row, center, was the Democratic party presidential nominee in 1920. O'Connell was unseated for a third term by James Michael Curley. (Courtesy of Lenahan O'Connell.)

Martin J. Lomasney (1859–1933), the political czar of Boston's West End, is captured in an enthusiastic gesture during a 1930 speech. Orphaned at age 11 and a former lamplighter and city health inspector, Lomasney served on the Board of Aldermen and in the state legislature. The classic ward boss, Lomasney could be found daily at his political headquarters, the Hendricks Club, organized in 1885, listening to constituents in need of work, medical assistance for a loved one, intervention on behalf of a youngster in trouble with the law, or help in paying overdue rent and butcher bills. (Courtesy of the *Boston Herald*.)

Bearing the caption, "The State House Chock Full of Hibernians," this drawing, mocking the Irish rise in politics, appeared in a Boston weekly in 1895. It features all the stock nativist caricatures of the Catholic clergy, Irish policeman, politician, and laborer—pawns of the satanic, foreign potentate, the pope.

"The Apostle of Sunshine," Mayor John F. Fitzgerald (1863–1950), left, poses with yachtsman and tea-maker Sir Thomas Lipton, 1912. Born in a tenement house in the North End, Fitzgerald hawked newspapers on the streets of Boston, attended Boston Latin School, and was forced to withdraw from Harvard Medical School after a year in order to help out his family, following his father's sudden death in 1885. Entering politics, the exuberant, outgoing Fitzgerald was elected to three terms in Congress and following the death of incumbent Patrick Collins in 1905, was elected mayor. Defeated for re-election, Fitzgerald rebounded in 1910, beating Boston Brahmin James Jackson Storrow by the slim margin of 1,400 votes. A political showman who serenaded voters with the song "Sweet Adeline," Fitzgerald was the maternal grandfather of President John F. Kennedy. (Courtesy of the Boston Public Library, Print Department.)

Mounted impressively on his steed, Mayor John F. Fitzgerald rides through the streets of Boston during the 1912 Saint Patrick's Day parade. (Courtesy of the Boston Public Library, Print Department.)

In March of 1912 President William Howard Taft, standing directly below the Society's banner, attended a banquet marking the 175th anniversary of the Charitable Irish Society of Boston at the Hotel Somerset. To the President's right is William Henry Cardinal O'Connell. The more than 800 people in attendance feasted on a menu that included Strained Chicken Gumbo, Mock Turtle Au Madere, Roast Jumbo Squab Au Cresson, and "Fancy Ice Cream." (Courtesy of the Archdiocese of Boston Archives.)

Prominent physician and Boston School Committeeman David D. Scannell (1875–1963) is seen leaving church with his bride, Elizabeth MacDonald, on Valentine's Day, 1912. Second generation Boston Irish, Scannell earned All-American baseball honors during his undergraduate days at Harvard College and graduated from Harvard Medical School in 1900. Like numerous physicians of his era, Dr. Scannell viewed it as his civic and professional duty to serve on the school committee, winning election for the first time in 1905. (Courtesy of Henry Scannell.)

Women's rights advocate Margaret Foley (1875–1957) spreads her message outside the Massachusetts State House, c. 1910. A former swimming and gymnastics instructor, Foley, "The Grand Heckler," criss-crossed Massachusetts during the 1914 gubernatorial campaign in an automobile known as the "Big Suffragette Machine," confronting at every rally candidates opposed to extending the vote to women. (Courtesy of Schlesinger Library, Radcliffe College.)

David I. Walsh (1872–1947), elected the first Catholic governor of Massachusetts in 1913, exhorts citizens on the Boston Common to join the armed forces during the First World War. Born in Leominster, Massachusetts, and a graduate of Holy Cross College and Boston University Law School, Walsh became the first Massachusetts Democrat to be elected to the United States Senate since antebellum days in 1918. (Courtesy of Holy Cross College Library.)

Senator Walsh, on the right, greets the great Irish tenor, John McCormack. Walsh was an ardent New Dealer and chairman of the powerful Senate Naval Affairs Committee, which investigated the Japanese attack on Pearl Harbor. Serving nearly 30 years in Washington, Walsh was defeated for a fifth term in 1946 by Republican Henry Cabot Lodge Jr. (Courtesy of Holy Cross College Library.)

Maurice J. Tobin (1901–1953), "Boston's Handsomest Mayor," and his bride, Helen Noonan, pose on their wedding day, 1932. Born on Mission Hill, Tobin quit school at the age of 16 to work for a leather firm and the telephone company, starting out as a cable splicer and progressing over 15 years to traffic manager. He attended law school, served in the state legislature and on the Boston School Committee, and in 1937 defeated James Michael Curley in a rancorously fought campaign for mayor. Elected governor of Massachusetts in 1944, Tobin was a champion of New Deal labor and social legislation and tried to persuade the newly formed United Nations to establish its headquarters in Boston. Defeated for re-election, Tobin was appointed secretary of labor by President Harry Truman in the summer of 1948. Tall, handsome, and well tailored, Tobin and patrician-looking Secretary of State Dean Acheson were regarded as the two best-dressed men in public life by the Washington press. In 1953, Tobin, only 52 years of age, suffered a fatal heart attack at his summer home in Scituate, Massachusetts. (Courtesy of the Boston Public Library, Print Department.)

Seen here *c.* 1934, Mayor Frederick W. Mansfield (1877–1958) was the son of Irish immigrants. A registered pharmacist before becoming a prominent labor attorney, he was president of the Massachusetts Bar Association in the 1920s and founded the Catholic Lawyers League to discourage fellow Catholic attorneys from handling divorce cases. Mayor of Boston from 1934 to 1938, Mansfield was an unelectrifying political personality—"as colorful as a lump of mud," according to one newspaperman. (Courtesy of the Boston Public Library, Print Department.)

A smiling Mayor Tobin, front row, left, and his attractive wife, Helen, stand with members of the Massachusetts delegation to the Democratic National Convention in Chicago, July 1940. Boston-born Paul A. Dever, the state's attorney general and later governor of Massachusetts, is to Tobin's immediate left. Between Tobin and Dever, wearing glasses, is Congressman John W. McCormack. (Courtesy of the Boston Public Library, Print Department.)

Eight

IRELAND FOREVER

In Boston and other major American cities, Irish immigrants supported the fight for Irish freedom by purchasing bonds issued by the Irish Republican Brotherhood, founded in Dublin in 1858 and committed to the armed overthrow of English rule in Ireland. This 1866 bond bears the likenesses of the Irish martyrs Robert Emmet and Theobald Wolfe Tone and shows Mother Erin entreating an Irish veteran of the American Civil War to pick up his saber on behalf of his native land. (Courtesy of the Massachusetts Historical Society.)

GRAND
Centennial Celebration

OF THE BIRTH OF

Robert Emmet,

Ireland's Martyr-Patriot.

" With thee were the dreams of my earliest love;
Every thought of my reason was thine;
In my last humble prayer to the Spirit above,
Thy name shall be mingled with mine.
Oh! blest are the lovers and friends who shall live
The days of thy glory to see;
But the next dearest blessing that Heaven can give
Is the pride of thus dying for thee."

The Irishmen of Boston, and all others who revere the memory of one of the noblest characters of the century, are invited to participate in the commemoration of the centenary of his birth, which will take place in

TREMONT TEMPLE, BOSTON,

Monday Evening, March 4, at 8 o'clock.

ROBERT EMMET, by his life, has set an example worthy of imitation, and, at his death, left to his countrymen a legacy which it is their duty to execute.

Hon. P. A. COLLINS will preside.

JOHN BOYLE O'REILLY, Esq.,

Will read A POEM written by him for the occasion.

AN ORATION

WILL BE DELIVERED BY

A. A. GRIFFIN, Esq., of New York.

Doors open at 7.30 P.M.

Admission, 25 Cents.   Reserved Seats, 50 Cents.

Duffy, Cashman & Co., Printers, 27 Boylston Street, Boston.

Tremont Temple was "filled with an appreciative audience" commemorating the 100th anniversary of the birth of "Ireland's martyr-patriot" Robert Emmet (1778–1803), reported the *Boston Pilot* in 1878. The youngest of 17 children and son of one of Ireland's leading physicians, Emmet was publicly hanged, drawn, quartered, and beheaded in Dublin in 1803 for leading an unsuccessful rebellion against the British Crown. Emmet's patriotic speech on the eve of his execution is regarded as a classic in the English language, stirring a young boy growing up in a log cabin in Kentucky named Abraham Lincoln. In his introductory remarks at Tremont Temple, Patrick Collins hailed Emmet as "Ireland's purist patriot." John Boyle O'Reilly, the ex-Fenian, read his poem dedicated to Emmet and, was in the words of the *Pilot* correspondent, "listened to throughout with riveted attention." The main speech of the evening by Anthony A. Griffin, an Irish nationalist and New York City educator, was "a gem of terse eloquence," wrote the *Pilot*. (Courtesy of Special Collections, Boston College.)

Michael Davitt (1846–1906), the father of the Land League movement in Ireland, was one in a long procession of prominent Irish nationalists to visit Boston in the decades immediately after the American Civil War. Davitt was evicted from his Mayo cottage as a child and lost his right arm at the age of ten in a Lancashire cotton factory accident. Joining the Fenian movement that was committed to the physical overthrow of British rule in Ireland, Davitt served seven years of hard labor in English prisons. Upon his release, Davitt in 1879 organized the Land League movement, urging his countrymen to throw off the yoke of "Landlordism" through parliamentary agitation, a national boycott of unfair rents, and protest against evictions. Combining forces with the great Charles Stewart Parnell in what came to be known in Irish politics as the "New Departure," the two men would shake Westminster to its very foundation in the 1880s. (Courtesy of the Library of Congress.)

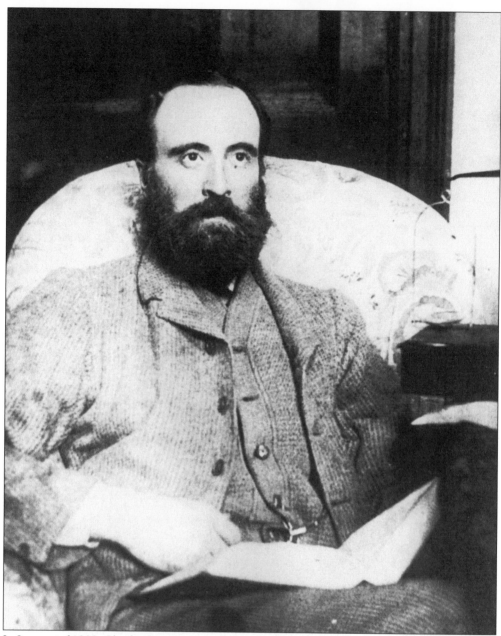

In January of 1880, Charles Stewart Parnell (1846–1891), the great agitator for Home Rule and land reform in Ireland, addressed a capacity crowd at the Boston Music Hall. In the audience, made up of "all classes of society," was Wendell Phillips, the old abolitionist, who exclaimed, "I have come here . . . from a keen desire to see the man that has forced John Bull to listen." Parnell, the son of an American mother and grandson of Commodore Charles Stewart, commander of the U.S.S. *Constitution* during the War of 1812, gave what the *Boston Globe* called "a plain, convincing statement of Ireland's woes and England's oppression." Parnell's national tour included an address before the U.S. House of Representatives. A love affair with Mrs. Kitty O'Shea, a married woman, precipitated Parnell's downfall in 1890, leaving the struggle for Irish freedom to yet another generation. (Courtesy of the Library of Congress.)

One of the few leaders of the 1916 Easter Rebellion in Dublin to escape a British firing squad, Eamon De Valera (1882–1975), president of the outlawed Irish Republic, arrives at South Station on Saturday evening, June 28, 1919, with some 50,000 people, the largest crowd in Boston history to ever turn out for a foreign dignitary, enthusiastically greeting him. The next day De Valera addressed an overflowing crowd of 60,000 at Fenway Park, poignantly making his opening remarks in Gaelic. (Courtesy of the *Boston Globe*.)

A mathematician by training and speaking with a "bit of a brogue," De Valera is welcomed to Boston by members of the reception committee. Born in New York City in 1882, the son of an Irish mother and Cuban father, De Valera spent 18 tumultuous months in the United States raising millions of dollars and trying without success to win official diplomatic recognition for the Irish Republic. (Courtesy of the *Boston Globe*.)

In October of 1849 the brig *Saint John*, five weeks out of Galway with 121 passengers and crew on board and captained by a man named Oliver, encountered fierce Northeast gales near the Massachusetts coast, slamming onto Grampus Rock off Cohasset, sending 99 to a watery grave on Sunday, October 7. Henry David Thoreau, on his way to Cape Cod, visited the rocky Cohasset beach strewn with battered corpses and timbers from the shipwreck, "so rotten," the Concord writer maintained, "that I could almost thrust my umbrella through them." On a radiantly beautiful Memorial Day in 1914, 10,000 people, "of all races and shades of religious belief," crowded into Cohasset Central Cemetery. Governor David I. Walsh was the featured speaker for the dedication of this magnificent 19-foot Celtic cross, erected by the Ancient Order of Hibernians, to 47 victims of the *Saint John* disaster. (Photograph by Greg Cecconi.)

Nine

FOLK HEROES AND LEGENDS

Ex-heavyweight champion John L. Sullivan (1858–1918), America's first national sports hero, converses with Jimmy Collins, player-manager of Boston's American League baseball team in 1904. (Courtesy of the Boston Public Library, Print Department.)

Born in the South End in 1858, Sullivan, shown here at the age of 19, was 5 feet 10 inches tall and weighed 180 pounds. His method of fighting, related a writer, "was simply to hammer his opponent into unconsciousness." In 1882, Sullivan, the "Terror of Terrors," defeated Paddy Ryan for the American Boxing Championship.

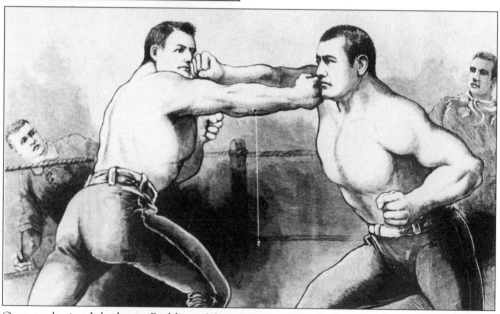

On a sweltering July day in Richburg, Mississippi, in 1889, Sullivan, right, dressed in "bright green tights," met Jake Kilrain in the last bare-knuckle fight for the American Boxing Championship. Sullivan, delivering "one terrible brain-shaker after another," knocked Kilrain down some 30 times and was declared the victor after 75 rounds. Three years later, overweight and breathing "like a huge porpoise," Sullivan lost his title to James Corbett. (*National Police Gazette.*)

Sullivan following his loss to Corbett worked as a vaudeville actor, starring as Simon Legree in *Uncle Tom's Cabin*, and to atone for years of riotous living joined the temperance movement. Sullivan squandered the fortune he made in prize-fighting, a $10,000 diamond-studded belt presented to him in 1887 by Boston admirers, ending up in a New York City pawnshop. In 1908 Sullivan divorced his first wife, a former chorus girl, and married Kate Harkins, left, a boyhood sweetheart. Widowed and living with an old sparring partner named George Bush, Sullivan died in February 1918. With " ten strong men" bearing his casket, he was buried at Old Calvary Cemetery in the Roslindale section of Boston, an imposing granite monument marking the grave site of the "Boston Strong Boy."

In 1868, John Boyle O'Reilly (1844–1890), a 24-year-old Fenian, was exiled to Australia for plotting rebellion against Great Britain. Aided by a local priest, O'Reilly, "Convict No. 9843," escaped from the penal colony 13 months later, finding passage during one leg of his long journey to freedom on a whaling vessel out of New Bedford. "Alive with genius," O'Reilly rose to fame as a poet, novelist, and editor of the *Boston Pilot*. (Courtesy of the *Boston Pilot*.)

O'Reilly was an eloquent champion of the Rights of Labor and condemned the mistreatment of the American Indian and recently emancipated slave. A romantic, engaging, manly figure, O'Reilly, more than any other person of his generation, also helped foster better understanding between Irish Catholics and Yankee Protestants. O'Reilly died at the age of 46 from an accidental overdose of pills in August of 1890 at his summer cottage in Hull, a fishing village south of Boston. (Courtesy of the Bostonian Society.)

Aptly described by one modern historian as a man "too formidable to be loved," William Henry Cardinal O'Connell (1859–1944), the son of an Irish mill worker from Lowell, Massachusetts, succeeded Archbishop John J. Williams as bishop of Boston in 1907. A graduate of Boston College, O'Connell was ordained in Rome in 1884. A born churchman, O'Connell, after a decade as a parish priest, served as rector of the American College at Rome, papal envoy to Japan, and bishop of Portland, Maine. The spiritual leader of some 1 million Catholics and a man of extraordinary executive ability, O'Connell was elevated to the Sacred College of Cardinals in 1911. He cast a long shadow over Boston's religious, civic, political, and social life for nearly 40 years. (Courtesy of the *Boston Pilot*.)

A 1915 Chickering photograph captures Cardinal O'Connell on his Episcopal throne at the Cathedral of the Holy Cross. His Eminence was held in great reverence by the laity, and politicians carefully studied his pronouncements on public issues up on Beacon Hill. O'Connell was chauffeured around in a Pierce Arrow automobile, upholstered in cardinal red, and had a summer cottage in the seashore Yankee enclave of Marblehead, north of Boston. Politically, the cardinal was suspected of being a Republican. (Courtesy of the Library of Congress.)

In the early years of his episcopacy Cardinal O'Connell lived in a granite mansion on Granby Street in the Back Bay, and beginning in 1915, on an estate on Aspinwill Hill in suburban Brookline. In the 1920s, using a portion of a $5-million fortune bequeathed to him by the Keith family, owners of a chain of vaudeville theaters, Cardinal O'Connell commissioned the architectural firm of Maginnis and Walsh to design the dignified "Archbishop's House," overlooking the grounds of Saint John's Seminary in Brighton. (Courtesy of the *Boston Herald*.)

Cardinal O'Connell confers with Major Henry Lee Higginson (1834–1919), investment banker, founder, and benefactor of the Boston Symphony Orchestra. O'Connell was a man of refinement and culture. He was fluent in several foreign languages, played the piano and organ, composed liturgical music, and attended the symphony regularly. Higginson, or "The Major" as he was known in State Street, was a calvary officer during the American Civil War. His right cheek bore the scar from a Confederate saber. (Courtesy of the Isabella Stewart Gardner Museum.)

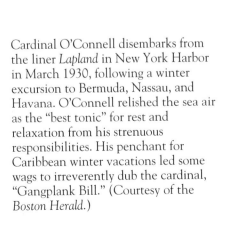

Cardinal O'Connell disembarks from the liner *Lapland* in New York Harbor in March 1930, following a winter excursion to Bermuda, Nassau, and Havana. O'Connell relished the sea air as the "best tonic" for rest and relaxation from his strenuous responsibilities. His penchant for Caribbean winter vacations led some wags to irreverently dub the cardinal, "Gangplank Bill." (Courtesy of the *Boston Herald*.)

President emeritus A. Lawrence Lowell of Harvard University stands with Cardinal O'Connell, both Olympian representatives of Yankee Protestant and Roman Catholic Boston. O'Connell, along with poet Robert Frost, received an honorary degree from Harvard in 1937. (Courtesy of the Archdiocese of Boston Archives.)

Mayor James Michael Curley (1874–1958), c. 1930, was the most flamboyant, tempestuous, resourceful, controversial, and resilient personality in 20th-century Massachusetts political history. He served four terms in the U.S. Congress, four terms as mayor of Boston, and a stormy two years as governor during the Great Depression. Curley, it should be noted, also served two months in the Suffolk County Jail for taking a post office examination for a constituent in 1902. He was incarcerated for five months in 1947, at the age of 72, at the federal prison in Danbury, Connecticut, following his conviction in a federal contract-awarding scheme during his time as a congressman in Washington during World War II. (Courtesy of the *Boston Herald*.)

Curley grew up in a cold-water tenement on Northampton Street in Roxbury, the neighborhood having one of the highest infant mortality and tuberculosis rates in the city. Visible in this rare 1870s photograph of Curley's old neighborhood are the buildings of the Boston City Hospital on Harrison Avenue. Off in the distance are masts of ships docked along the wharves of South Bay, which Curley nostalgically recalled a half-century later in his autobiography. (Courtesy of the Boston City Hospital.)

Curly first ran for public office in 1897. His Tammany Club, a political organization that sponsored family outings, annual balls, and athletic teams and delivered turkeys at Christmastime and coal in the winter to neighbors down on their luck, made him the undisputed boss of Ward 17 in Roxbury. (Courtesy of Holy Cross College Library.)

Curley "is an essentially dominant man, compelling, personal and vital," maintained a Boston reporter in 1905. After serving on the Common Council and Board of Aldermen and as a state legislator and congressman, Curley was elected to his first term as mayor of Boston in 1913. (Courtesy of the Boston Public Library, Print Department.)

Curley speaks at Marine Park in South Boston, 1917. Curley was artful, intelligent, a man of boundless energy and possessed a magnetic, charming personality and rich, sonorous voice. Forced to leave school at the age of 14, he educated himself by reading Dickens, Hugo, Dumas, and "a lot of Shakespeare." He polished his public speaking by enrolling in evening classes at the Staley College of the Spoken Word during his days on the Boston Common Council. (Courtesy of Holy Cross College Library.)

On Saint Patrick's Day, 1915, workers began building Mayor Curley's 21-room brick mansion with its fabled Shamrock Shutters on the Jamaicaway. Situated on 2 acres of land, the home "was better than anything on Beacon Street," contends one Curley biographer. It had a beautiful mahogany-paneled dining room, mahogany doors, Italian marble fireplaces, a winding staircase, a bronze two-story chandelier from an embassy in Washington, five bathrooms, and a heated garage. (Courtesy of the Boston Public Library, Print Department.)

Mayor Curley and his wife, Mary, vacation in Palm Beach, Florida, 1926. Mary Emelda Hurlihy was a member of a female singing group, the "Creole Belles," from Curley's neighborhood of Roxbury. The couple was married at Saint Francis de Sales Church in Roxbury on June 27, 1906. Mary, or Mae, as she was sometimes called, was gracious and discerning, giving sound political counsel to her husband. (Courtesy of the *Boston Herald*.)

Curley relaxes with his family in 1924. Mrs. Curley died of cancer in June of 1930, six months into her husband's third term as mayor. Curley was a loving husband and father and knew tragedy first-hand, surviving seven of his nine children. (Courtesy of the *Boston Herald*.)

Curley was the first big city mayor to endorse Franklin D. Roosevelt, left, for president in 1932. Curley took out a $25,000 mortgage on his Jamaicaway mansion, campaigned 8,000 miles, giving 141 speeches in 22 states on behalf of Roosevelt. In what Curley termed in his memoirs as the "Betrayal," the wily Roosevelt denied him the patrician post of secretary of the navy, as well as his second choice of ambassador to Italy. (Courtesy of the Boston Public Library, Print Department.)

Curley married Gertrude Casey Dennis on January 7, 1937, just hours before he officially relinquished his duties as governor of the Commonwealth. Twenty years younger than the governor, Mrs. Dennis was a widow with two young sons and was a professional singer and pianist. "No woman could have helped falling in love with him," Mrs. Curley affectionately noted. "He just swept me off my feet. We were both in our teens again." (Courtesy of the *Boston Herald*.)

Ten

THE CHANGING
OF THE GUARD

William Cardinal O'Connell lays in funeral state at the Cathedral of the Holy Cross, April 28, 1944. In poor health for years, O'Connell died at his residence in Brighton, and during five days of obsequies at the old stone Cathedral, thousands filed past the cardinal's bier, his red *galero* resting at his feet. His Eminence, a Boston newspaper fittingly noted, "was the sort of figure who comes forth only at long intervals." (Courtesy of the Boston Public Library, Print Department.)

Tall, rugged-looking, with an inimitable gravelly voice, Richard J. Cushing (1895–1970) succeeded the urbane, aloof, aristocratic Cardinal O'Connell as bishop of Boston. Born in South Boston of Irish parents, Cushing was beloved for his human warmth and congeniality. Elevated to cardinal in 1958, Cushing was at the forefront of the modern ecumenical movement, uniting Catholics, Protestants, and Jews in a spirit of prayer, brotherhood, and understanding. (Courtesy of the *Boston Pilot*.)

Archbishop Cushing tries his hand at the bagpipes. A prolific builder and incomparable fund-raiser, Cushing during his 25-year episcopacy built some 80 new churches and numerous shrines, schools, colleges, orphanages, hospitals, residences for the elderly, a school for the mentally retarded on whose grounds he is buried, and a seminary for delayed priestly vocations. He also brought, through the modern marvel of television, the spiritual sustenance of daily Mass to many confined to their homes. (Courtesy of the *Boston Pilot*.)

Cushing was at ease in the world of politics. He was an intimate friend of the Kennedy family, delivering the invocation at President John Kennedy's inauguration in 1961. In this 1947 photograph, Cushing greets, from left to right, three descendants of the Pilgrim fathers: Senator Leverett Saltonstall, Senator Henry Cabot Lodge Jr., and Massachusetts governor Robert Fiske Bradford. To the far right is Mayor John B. Hynes. (Courtesy of the Archdiocese of Boston Archives.)

The post–World War II era was the golden age of American Catholicism. In October of 1947, the Holy Name Society of the United States convened in Boston, some 130,000 men parading through the streets, taking eight hours to pass the reviewing stand in what one newspaper called "the greatest religious demonstration in the history of New England." Members are shown here at a Holy Hour at Braves Field. (Courtesy of the Archdiocese of Boston Archives.)

In September of 1946 three generations of Boston Irish politicians, the old political war-horse, Mayor James M. Curley, left, the tall, meticulously-dressed Governor Maurice J. Tobin, center, and congressional candidate, John F. Kennedy, right, in his naval uniform, appeared on the speakers' platform at the Boston Arena for the opening session of the annual convention of the Veterans of Foreign Wars. Kennedy, son of Ambassador Joseph P. Kennedy and a PT boat commander in the Pacific, was general chairman of the convention. The battleship *Missouri* was anchored in Boston Harbor, incidentally, during the convention. (Courtesy of the Boston Public Library, Print Department.)

In the waning days of the historic 1948 presidential election, Harry S. Truman campaigns in Boston. Seated next to the President is Maurice Tobin, appointed secretary of labor two months earlier by Truman, and Paul A. Dever, the successful Democratic candidate for governor. In front are Congressman John McCormack and Mayor Curley. (Courtesy of the Boston Public Library, Print Department.)

James Michael Curley died on Wednesday, November 12, 1958, at the Boston City Hospital, a few blocks from the humble tenement in which he was born some 83 years earlier. He lay in state at the august Hall of Flags in the State House for two days, the wedding band of his father, Michael, on his left hand. He was buried from the Cathedral of the Holy Cross, the Requiem Mass being said by his youngest child, Father Francis Xavier Curley, a Jesuit priest. The mayor's wake and funeral, attended by more than a million people from all walks of life, was "a spectacle unparalleled in the Bay State's 300 year history," noted the *Christian Science Monitor*. (Courtesy of the *Boston Herald*.)

Edwin O'Connor, the author of the 1956 classic, *The Last Hurrah*, believed by many to be based on Curley's turbulent political career, pays his final respects to the mayor. Born in Providence, Rhode Island, in 1918, O'Connor graduated from Notre Dame University in 1939 and served with the U.S. Coast Guard in Boston during World War II. The best-selling *The Last Hurrah* and a movie based on the novel made O'Connor wealthy overnight. A devout Catholic and warm human being, O'Connor died at the age of 50 in 1968. (Courtesy of the *Boston Herald*.)

Curley's gravestone at Old Calvary Cemetery in Roslindale delineates the various public offices he held and bears the title he cherished most: "The Mayor of the Poor." Curley during his 50 years in politics provided work for the down-and-out and improved the lot of ordinary citizens by building parks, playgrounds, beaches, bathhouses, schools, libraries, hospitals, neighborhood health clinics, and municipal buildings. (Courtesy of the *Boston Herald*.)

Appointed to run the city temporarily after Mayor Curley was sentenced to jail in 1946 for mail fraud, John B. Hynes (1897–1970), a career civil servant, defeated his old boss—who had been pardoned after five months in prison by President Harry S. Truman—in the mayoral race of 1949. An efficient executive whose quiet manner of doing things earned him the nickname of "Whispering Johnny," Hynes initiated unprecedented urban renewal projects that drastically altered the skyline of Boston. (Courtesy of the *Boston Herald*.)

Crippled by polio four years earlier, John F. Collins (1919–1995) was elected the 44th mayor of Boston in 1959. Reared in Roxbury where his father played on Mayor Curley's old Tammany Club baseball team, Collins graduated from law school in 1941, finishing first in his class and at the outbreak of World War II, joining the army and rising from private to captain. Handsome, forceful, and pragmatic, Collins is shown here studying one of his many urban renewal plans. (Courtesy of the *Boston Herald*.)

John W. McCormack (1891–1980), the future Speaker of the U.S. House of Representatives, poses in his World War I uniform. Born in South Boston, McCormack was forced to quit school at the age of 13 in order to help support his widowed mother and two younger brothers. Elected to Congress in 1928, McCormack was an ardent New Dealer and played an important role in the passage of the landmark Social Security Act of 1935. (Courtesy of the Mugar Library, Boston University.)

M. Harriet Joyce, wife of John McCormack, appears in her bridal gown, 1920. A native of South Boston, Mrs. McCormack was an accomplished contralto, performing with the Metropolitan Opera Company. The McCormacks, who had no children, were married for 51 years. Their devotion to one another became a "Washington Legend"; no matter how pressing his legislative duties, Congressman McCormack never failed in over four decades in the nation's capital to have dinner with his beloved Harriet. (Courtesy of the Mugar Library, Boston University.)

A fiery partisan debater, legislative horse trader, and parliamentarian, McCormack, "The fighting Irishman from South Boston," moved steadily up the democratic congressional leadership ladder in the 1930s and 1940s. In 1962, following the death of the renowned Sam Rayburn of Texas, the 71-year-old McCormack was elected the first Roman Catholic Speaker of the House of Representatives. A tall, lean, white-haired figure, who smoked cigars and enjoyed playing poker, Speaker McCormack dressed in conservative dark suits—the pockets, noted a reporter, "always bulging with notes, programs, bills, and reference material." McCormack retired in 1970 after 42 years in Congress, sentimentally noting, "My heart is in this House." (Courtesy of the *Boston Herald*.)

John Kennedy listens attentively to his wealthy and controversial father, Joseph P. Kennedy (1888–1969), *c*. 1947. Educated at Boston Latin School and Harvard College, Mr. Kennedy married Rose Fitzgerald, the daughter of Mayor John F. Fitzgerald and belle of Boston Irish Catholic society, in 1914. He amassed a fortune as a banker, Wall Street speculator, Hollywood moviemaker, and by astute investments in real estate and the liquor import business. From 1938 to 1940, Joseph Kennedy served as the American ambassador to Great Britain. (Courtesy of the Boston Public Library, Print Department.)

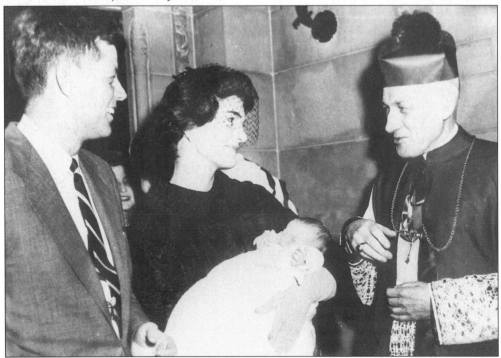

Senator Kennedy, his wife, Jacqueline, holding their infant daughter, Caroline, engage in conversation with Archbishop Cushing, 1957. (Courtesy of the *Boston Pilot*.)

John F. Kennedy (1917–1963) concludes his grueling 50,000-mile campaign for the White House at the Boston Garden on election eve, November 7, 1960. More than 1 million people lined the route of Kennedy's cavalcade from the airport through downtown Boston. Kennedy, dressed in a blue suit, approached the stage at the Garden at exactly 9:51 p.m, the crowd of 25,000 breaking out in a "ear-splitting roar" as streamers and confetti cascaded from the balconies and a band struck up "Anchors Aweigh." "This is the warmest welcome I have received in a long campaign," declared a grateful and smiling Kennedy. Bathed by searchlights, Kennedy in a 20-minute speech, punctuated by applause after applause, attacked the Republican Party policies of the past. With characteristic vigor, he asserted, "I run for the Presidency of the United States because it is the center of action." The next day, November 8, 1960, John Fitzgerald Kennedy was elected the first Catholic president of the United States, defeating Republican Richard M. Nixon by just 112,000 popular votes. (Courtesy of the Boston Public Library, Print Department.)

ACKNOWLEDGMENTS

The author has met many generous and accommodating souls during the course of researching and writing this book. My deepest appreciation to attorney Jim Marsh, a loyal and precious friend since boyhood; photographer Gregory Cecconi, who faithfully accompanied me on my pilgrimages to more than 50 libraries, historical societies, parish churches, rectories, and other repositories, and skillfully assisted me in arranging these rare images and illustrations; Sinclair Hitchings, Keeper of Prints, Boston Public Library, and his conscientious assistant, Aaron Schmidt; Sally Pierce of the Boston Athenaeum and Harry Katz of the Library of Congress; John Cronin, Librarian, *Boston Herald*; Doug Southard and Pat Crawford, Bostonian Society; Grace O'Neil; Father Laurence W. McGrath, Librarian, Saint John's Seminary, Brighton; Librarian Jim Mahoney of Holy Cross College; Stephen Gawlik of the *Boston Pilot*; Professor David P. Twomey of Boston College; Henry F. Scannell, Microtext Department, Boston Public Library; Jim O'Toole and Tim Meagher, both former archivists of the Arch-Diocese of Boston; the late Sister Dorothea Furfey of the Sisters of Notre Dame; Bill Hourihan, Ph.D., of Columbia, South Carolina, a historian's historian; Sister Grace Collins of the Carney Hospital of Dorchester; Meg L. Winslow, Curator, Mount Auburn Cemetery, Cambridge; Rebecca Reynolds of Forest Hills Cemetery, Boston; Brenda Hamilton, Librarian, Massachusetts State Library, Boston; Robert Severy, Armand Amadei, Amy Kaufman, Lenahan O'Connell, Anthony Sammarco, Jim Fahey, and Bob Feeney; John McColgan, Archivist for the City of Boston; Librarian Mary Jo Campbell of the Boston Public Library at Lower Mills, Dorchester; and Robert O'Neil, Director of the John J. Burns Library, Boston College.

This book is dedicated to my brother Martin with inexpressible love and affection.